IF YOU KEEP PUTTING OFF UNTIL
TOMORROW ... *OVERCOMING
PROCRASTINATION* CAN HELP YOU
TODAY!

It will open your eyes to just what makes you
late in everything from writing a paper to filing
a tax return to making a sexual advance.

It will teach you not only to understand your
particular problem, but how to definitely do
something about it with simple and specific
actions.

It will give you Dr. Albert Ellis' total strategy
for conquering not only procrastination but
life's other difficulties.

And above all, it will show you exactly how to
take your time and your life out of the power of
irrational forces and feelings, and put them where
they belong—under your control.

OVERCOMING
PROCRASTINATION

SIGNET and MENTOR Books of Related Interest

Overcoming Procrastination

or

How to Think and Act Rationally in Spite of Life's Inevitable Hassles

Albert Ellis, Ph.D.
and
William J. Knaus, Ed.D.

A SIGNET BOOK

NEW AMERICAN LIBRARY

TIMES MIRROR

SIGNET, SIGNET CLASSICS, MENTOR, PLUME, MERIDIAN AND NAL BOOKS
are published by The New American Library, Inc.,
1633 Broadway, New York, New York 10019

First Signet Printing, July, 1979

5   6   7   8   9   10   11

PRINTED IN THE UNITED STATES OF AMERICA

Dedicated to

the hundreds of our clients
who used to procrastinate
but seldom do any more,
with great gratitude
for what we learned from them.

Contents

Introduction

How many college-level individuals procrastinate? Often? Seriously? No one seems to know. Incredibly, this important question has not inspired many factual studies. Our guess? About ninety-five percent.

"Really?" you ask. "As many as that?"

Yes, as far as we can judge. In our general observations of the human species and especially in our work as psychotherapists, we have run across innumerable procrastinators. And their numbers increase!

Not only students, of course. Writers notoriously delay getting their manuscripts to editors on time. Business men and women submit literally millions of late reports each year. Applicants for jobs, school openings, civil service exams, and almost everything else under the sun—again by the millions, maybe even billions—promise themselves to fill out the necessary forms promptly, then finish them at the last minute, or send them in days or weeks after deadline . . . or not at all.

Do people really procrastinate with forms when it will cost them money? Oh, yes! Who among us has not mailed tax forms at the very last minute—and considerably after that? And how many human beings avoid being late most of the time for appointments, dates, dinners, interviews, therapy sessions, and whatnot? Damned few!

What about how-to books? Surely you can learn from copious literature how to overcome procrastination? Nope. The closest thing we could find in print was a book by Paul T. Ringenbach, *Procrastination Through the Ages, a Definitive History*. It presents an interesting survey, but it sheds little light on coping with the problem.

Does no one care? Will no one lift a finger to help rid the world of this destructive aspect of slothfulness? Fortunately we do and we will. For we don't like procrastination. It adds little to and it subtracts a lot from joyous, autonomous living. We don't see it as the worst emotional plague imaginable but we view it as a dangerous disadvantage. Part of the human condition—yes—but a nasty, unattractive part. And one that merits extirpation.

"But really?" you ask. "Can you actually *cure* procrastinators? Truly help them get off their rumps and stop delaying?"

We think we can. Not completely, of course. After spending some forty years, between the two of us, as psychotherapists, we don't feel sure that we can fully cure any troubled person. For some disturbance seems inherent in the human condition. People have pronounced biological and learned tendencies to act neurotically, to stay immature, and to defeat their best interests in important and powerful ways. As therapists, we think we often—indeed, usually—help them make significant emotional changes for the better: to enjoy themselves distinctly more and sabotage themselves considerably less. We can proudly say that our record, along with that of many other rational-emotive and cognitive-behavior therapists, stands second to none in this respect.

For rational-emotive therapy (RET, for short) pursues criteria of efficiency. It aims to bring about the most elegant and enduring forms of improvement for the highest proportion of clients with a minimum expenditure of their time and energy—and their therapist's. Rational, in economics, means efficient; and that stands as one of its main meanings in RET.

Rational-emotive therapy deals with all kinds of emotional problems, from mild neurosis to severe psychosis, and from everyday problems to esoteric disturbances. Stressing prevention as well as cure, it emphasizes an educational approach to common difficulties. Consequently it goes beyond the usual realm of treating phobias, obsessions, compulsions, and other severe troubles into the more mundane area of procrastination, avoidance of responsibility, and low frustration tolerance.

Again with good results. One of us (A.E.) has treated literally hundreds of inveterate procrastinators during his therapeutic career, and has given dozens of talks and workshops dealing with this subject. The co-author (W.K.) has treated hundreds of procrastinators and has made it his special bailiwick, at the Institute for Rational Living in New York and the Ft. Lee Consultation Center in New Jersey, to give procrastination workshops for both lay people and professionals. Both of us combined have probably talked to more people about their self-defeating tendencies to postpone and delay important projects than any other two therapists in history. Although we do many things in the field of psychotherapy, including training and supervising other rational therapists, the treatment of procrastination remains one of our specialties and we immodestly claim a high degree of authoritativeness in this area. Hence our decision to write this book.

We have yet another motive. We like to see RET applied to as many important areas of life as possible. Comprising as it does a scientific attitude toward problem-solving and a philosophical approach to uprooting virtually all forms of needless unhappiness, RET has significant applications in many areas. Though still a relatively young form of therapy and counseling, it has already made a name for itself in diverse fields. Thus, in the area of clinical psychotherapy, we have RET-oriented books by Aaron Beck (*Cognitive Therapy and the Emotional Disorders*), Albert Ellis (*Reason and Emotion in Psychotherapy, Growth Through Reason,* and *Humanistic Psychotherapy: The Rational-Emotive Approach*), Harold Greenwald (*Direct Decision Therapy*), Robert A. Harper (*The New Psychotherapies*), Arnold A. Lazarus (*Behavior Therapy and Beyond* and *Multimodal Therapy,* Donald Meichenbaum (*Cognitive Behavior Modification*), and Kenneth T. Morris and H. Mike Kanitz (*Rational-Emotive Therapy*).

In the area of general self-help, we have RET books by Daniel Blazier (*Poor Me, Poor Marriage*), Albert Ellis (*How to Master Your Fear of Flying and How to live with a "Neurotic"*), Albert Ellis and Robert A. Harper (*A Guide to Successful Marriage* and *A New Guide to Rational Living*), David Goodman and Maxie C. Maultsby, Jr. (*Emotional Well-Being Through Rational Behavior Training*), Martin Grossack (*You Are Not Alone*), Paul Hauck (*Overcoming Depression, Overcoming Frustration and Anger, Overcoming Worry and Fear*), Gerald Kranzler (*You Can Change How You Feel*), John Lembo (*Help Yourself*), Maxie Maultsby, Jr. (*More Personal Happiness Through Rational Self-Counseling* and *Help Yourself to Happiness*), Rian McMullin and Bill Casey (*Talk Sense to Yourself*), and Howard Young (*A Rational Counseling Primer*).

In the area of emotional education, childhood, and adolescence, we have books by Stweart Bedford (*Instant Replay*), Terry Berger (*I Have Feelings*), Edward Garcia and Nina Pellegrini (*Homer the Homely Hound Dog*), William J. Knaus (*Rational Emotive Education*), Albert Ellis, Janet L.

Wolfe, and Sandra Moseley (*How to Raise an Emotionally Healthy, Happy Child*), and Donald J. Tosi (*Toward Personal Growth: a Rational-Emotive Approach*).

In the realm of law and criminality, we have Albert Ellis's and John M. Gullo's *Murder and Assassination* and a forthcoming book by Virginia Anne Church.

In the realm of religion, we have Paul A. Hauck's *Reason in Pastoral Counseling* and another forthcoming book by Virginia Anne Church.

In the realm of sex and courtship, we have books by Albert Ellis (*The Art and Science of Love, Homosexuality, The Intelligent Woman's Guide to Mate-Hunting, The Sensuous Person, Sex and the Liberated Man*, and *Sex Without Guilt*) and by Albert Ellis and Edward Sagarin (*Nymphomania: A Study of the Oversexed Woman*).

In the field of leadership and management, we have Albert Ellis's *Executive Leadership: A Rational Approach.*

As the fields to which RET applies increase in number and scope, we think the problem of procrastination definitely merits its inclusion. So we have prepared this book on its causes and treatment and present it as the most comprehensive, and in some ways the only, work in its field. RET marches on!

This volume represents a pioneer presentation in at least one other important respect. RET consists of one of the few systematic applications of principles of general semantics to the field of psychotherapy—as E. Scott Baudhuin, Donald Meichenbaum, and Donald Mosher have shown. It hypothesizes that if people closely adhered to some of the rules laid down by Alfred Korzybski and spoke and thought with semantic precision—especially by omitting overgeneralizations from their descriptions—they would avoid much irrational thinking and enjoy greater emotional health.

To help along this process of encouraging humans to think more precisely, I (A.E.) have written three books and a good many articles in E-prime—a form of English developed by Korzybski's follower, D. David Bourland, Jr. The name E-prime comes from the semantic equation: E-prime = E minus *e*: where E represents all the words of standard English and *e* represents all the forms of *to be*: such as *is, was, am, has been, being*, etc. As Bourland has noted, this new usage has several advantages:

1. We eliminate certain meaningless and essentially unanswerable questions, such as, "What *is* my destiny?" and "Who *am* I?" For although you can sensibly answer such questions

as, "What do I like?" or "What thoughts and feelings do I have?" you cannot very well answer a vague question like, "Who *am* I?"

2. We forego some misleading abbreviations, such as, "We know this is the right thing to do." Such abbreviations involve the "is" of predication, and use vague referents like *this* which have no very clear meaning. We make much more sense when we say, "We have evidence that we'd better turn the steering wheel to the right when we want to avoid a car approaching us on the left."

3. We reveal some normally hidden sources of information and feelings. If we say, "It has been found that," we don't know *who* has found it. We'd better say, "Jones, in his study of polar bears, found that. . . ." If we say, "That's where it's at," we make a vague or meaningless statement. Better: "I believe that if you keep coming in late to work, your boss will fire you."

4. We tend to expand our awareness of our linguistic environment and we help ourselves find means for improving conditions in that environment. "My parents were the source of my troubles and still are" serves as a cop-out for your past and present behaviors. If you acknowledge, instead, "My parents kept criticizing me severely during my childhood, and I took them too seriously and thereby upset myself; now I *still* down myself when I hear them criticize me, and I consequently still feel worthless," you imply what you can and had better do to interrupt and change the self-downing tendencies that you *accepted* from the teachings of your parents.

5. We eliminate the feeling of completeness and finality implied when we use any form of the verb *to be*. We thereby forego the "is" of prediction and the use of such misleading statements and overgeneralization as "Procrastinators are fools"—which strongly implies (a) people who procrastinate always and invariably do so; (b) they never act unfoolishly when they engage in procrastination; and (c) they seem doomed to procrastinate and to behave foolishly at all times in the future. How misleading!

6. When we stick to E-prime and avoid all forms of *to be*, we discourage absolutistic self-fulfilling prophecies, such as, "I am a failure." For this non-E-prime sentence implies (a) I have always failed; (b) I will only and always fail in the future; and (c) the universe has a horror of my failing and will punish and damn me, perhaps for all eternity for failing.

In RET, we teach people to avoid the kinds of overgeneralizations that E-prime avoids. Many RET and RBT (rational behavior therapy) practitioners, especially Maxie C. Maultsby, Jr., have emphasized this point. Thus, when clients state, "I *must* work harder," we help them change that to, *"It would prove better* if I worked harder." When they say, "I *can't* stop worrying," we object, "You probably *can* stop worrying, but so far you haven't." When they insist, "I *always* do badly *every* time I go to a social affair," we urge them to change this to, "I *usually* do badly *much* of the time I go to a social affair."

Again, when people insist, "It would prove *awful* if I failed this course," we try to get them to say and think, "I would find it highly *inconvenient* if I failed this course." And, instead of "I *am* a bad person for acting so incompetently," we prefer, "I find it highly unfortunate when I act incompetently, but my incompetence does not make me a *bad person.*"

In many ways, then, RET uses semantic principles; and in this pioneering book on how to overcome procrastination, we consistently employ E-prime, which encourages the use of such principles. With the help of Robert H. Moore, a staff member of the Florida Branch of the Institute for Rational Living, Inc., at Clearwater, we have eliminated all the forms of *to be* and *to become* except in the dialogue quoted from our clients. Of course, we do not claim that our use of E-prime eliminates *all* kinds of overgeneralizations, but it certainly helps.

Do you procrastinate more than you would like? Do you have friends and associates who constantly sabotage their work and happiness by postponing activities they have promised to perform? Can you learn simple, practical measures to overcome self-defeating delay? Read on!

1. What Procrastination Means

Technically, procrastination means putting off something until a future time—postponing or deferring action on something you have decided to do. But, as everyone appears to sense, it has come to mean something quite different. In its generally understood definition, when you procrastinate you almost invariably go through several important steps:

1. You wish to do something, or at least agree to do it even though it intrinsically does not appeal to you, because you desire some favorable result that probably will ensue if you do this thing.

2. You make a definite decision to do it.

3. You needlessly delay doing it.

4. You observe the disadvantages or lack of advantages of delay.

5. You still postpone doing the thing you decided to do.

6. You berate yourself for procrastinating (or you defend yourself against self-downing by rationalizing or pushing the project out of your mind).

7. You continue to procrastinate.

8. You finish the project barely on time by making a last-minute rush to complete it, or you finish it late, or you never finish it.

9. You feel uncomfortable about your lateness and berate yourself for your unnecessary delay.

10. You assure yourself that such procrastination will not happen again, and that this time you really mean it!

11. Not too long afterward, especially if you have a complicated, difficult, and time-consuming project to complete, you procrastinate again.

As we shall show later in this book, not all procrastination follows that pattern. Some of it falls into the "normal" or healthy range—consists of legitimate delay that actually may help you complete certain projects more satisfactorily. But rarely! Most procrastinating has a clear-cut element of disturbance: It consists of an emotional problem and has distinctly self-defeating aspects (as virtually all emotional problems do). It stems from irrational choices. It includes a degree of compulsiveness. It brings poor and inefficient results. And, instead of leading to self-correction, it more often than not evolves as a pernicious habit that tends to perpetuate itself and develop into a vicious cycle of procrastination leading to self-damnation which leads to more procrastination.

Face it, then! Most procrastination constitutes an emotional hang-up that does you considerable damage. While hardly fatal—it merely impedes but seldom halts your functioning—it has enormous sabotaging effects.

Statistically, of course, it appears quite normal. Few people rarely resort to it; most of us practice it continually. But such prevalent behavior as overeating or cigarette smoking—and rationalizing—retains its popularity in innumerable times and climes. Which hardly proves that behavior harmless or good!

We shall discuss rationalization later, and show how you often keep your procrastination inviolate by resorting to various excuses—few of which hold water and most of which add havoc to your life. For when you procrastinate, you tend to deny that you do so. Or promise yourself that you will stop it tomorrow. Or refuse to admit some of the disadvantages that accrue from doing it.

But not always. You often consciously *know* you have no good excuse for engaging in needless and foolish delay; you *know* you could get off your butt and do what you have told yourself (and others) you would do; and you *know* you will bring about poor results if you continue to procrastinate. No matter! You *still* procrastinate . . . and procrastinate . . . and procrastinate.

Why? Because (at least in this regard) you have an emotional disturbance. You don't go completely off the wall. You don't do *everything* crazily. You won't end up in the looney bin. But you do have a clear-cut emotional problem—sometimes a severe one. Admit it—you do!

What can you do about it? Read on!

Some Typical Procrastinators

Al, a twenty-five-year-old student, wants his undergraduate degree, but doesn't read and study for exams. He has already dropped out of three colleges, has many incomplete grades on his transcripts, and chronically devaluates himself for taking so long to complete degree requirements.

Robert, a forty-year-old Ph.D. candidate in literature, feels depressed because he thinks he'll "never make it." He stalls writing his dissertation and the novel he has promised himself to do.

Gail, a twenty-four-year-old social worker, feels self-disgust for delaying decisions about where to live, about writing letters and returning phone calls, and about initiating new and exciting activities.

Thirteen-year-old Paul keeps thinking he would like to clean up part of the cellar at his parents' house in order to make a game room. He has contemplated this for the past three years and, rather than getting started, he tries not to think about the long-delayed project because when he reminds himself to do some work he lambastes himself for the time he already has "wasted."

These four individuals consistently delay projects they think highly worthwhile. This procrastination has at least two unpleasant consequences: First, the tasks stay undone and the advantages of completing them remain unsavored; second, those who procrastinate tend to denigrate themselves.

The majority report self-inflicted mental torture, indicated by statements like this: "I have no self-respect," "I *should* stop procrastinating, but I just can't. I feel so weak!" "A person like me has no future." "I can't do this. If I try, people will find out how stupid I am, so why bother?" "Here I go again, doing nothing. Poor sick me—what a poor excuse for a person! I feel so anxious!" "I'll never change, but some day I'll wish I had!" Such self-statements lead to feelings of depression, guilt, anxiety, panic, remorse, loneliness, helplessness, worthlessness, and loss of control.

Worry and self-recrimination hardly help you overcome procrastination; if self-inflicted threats worked, people would rarely procrastinate. Constant self-downing, on the other hand, can increase the likelihood of somatic difficulties, such as chronic fatigue, headaches, sleep problems, hypertension, and ulcers. Even when these physical symptoms do not appear, you may experience such adverse emotional consequences that you strongly desire to rid yourself of this problem.

Mere desire won't help! Nor will recrimination! The problem, when habitual, requires much work to uproot. *Persistent* work. Clearing up a series of incomplete tasks in the present won't guarantee against work piling up in the future. You will heighten your efficiency by committing yourself to a lifelong project of countering time wastage with purposeful effort. Yes, lifelong!

The habit of procrastination stems from a self-defeating philosophy. To help you understand and reduce the problem, let's examine the following case.

A Day in the Life of One Who Procrastinates

Maude opened her big brown eyes when the electric alarm went off. "Time to get up and get going! Oh, but not . . . just . . . yet!" She punched in the button to stop the noise, then snuggled back into her warm bed to avoid the cold fall morning chill. Soon her phone began to ring. Startled, she flew out of bed to answer it, and heard her friend Judy's cheerful voice greeting her, then somberly warning her to arrive on time for the car pool, as her lateness created great inconvenience. Her fellow travelers sometimes did not get to work on time because of her lateness. Maude grunted acknowledgment, swore she would arrive at the corner before the car got there, hung up the phone, and splashed water on her face in the hope of waking up.

She admired herself in the mirror, dried her face, and walked toward the kitchen past the pile of newspapers she had decided to throw out months ago, noting that some had yellowed and the heap had grown unmanageably huge. In fact, it towered above her head and she vowed she would definitely do something about it the coming weekend. Relieved that she soon would take care of the pile, she walked into the kitchen and remembered she had promised herself the night before that she would wash the dishes which had accumulated in the past several days. No time for that though. The car pool came first!

She breakfasted gloomily as she stared at the pile of food-encrusted dishes and began to think how much she hated her apartment and herself for putting off so many tasks. She concluded she couldn't stand her chronic procrastination and its effect on her life.

Maude left her apartment feeling helpless and hopeless. While walking to the corner, she mulled over her job and how much she disliked teaching young children, then realized she had left behind the lesson plan she had written the night before. "At least I did *that*!" she thought. Despite her dislike for her profession, she consistently prepared for each school day, and acted responsibly and conscientiously about her work with the children. She returned to her apartment to retrieve the lessons, and once again showed up late for the car pool, but not so late as to anger the other members.

On the way to work, she grumbled as usual about the ineffectiveness of the school's administrators, her lack of male companionship, and other dissatisfactions. The riders tended to ignore her and she began to feel even more upset, as it seemed nobody liked her. Actually, they had heard her complaints so many times that most had stopped listening because she always responded with a "yes-but" and never followed through on their suggestions. Since she refused to make herself available to meet men, and would not stand up for herself with the administration, her friends no longer concerned themselves with these issues.

To sum up: Maude procrastinates in many aspects of her life. She puts off seeking companionship, managing domestic chores, and doing other important projects. Day after day she suffers anguish about what she doesn't do.

She hardly has a unique problem. Millions of other Maudes procrastinate—and thereby suffer—too. In fact, almost everyone does!

Three Kinds of Procrastination

We can conveniently divide Maude's problems into three overlapping categories: self-development, personal maintenance, and irresponsibility to others.

Self-development refers to seeking and trying to attain desired and realistic goals. Maude wanted to involve herself with a man she could lovingly care for, and to find satisfaction in a career. But she did not focus her efforts on constructively working toward these goals and avoided taking the sound advice that others gave her.

Personal maintenance refers to doing those chores that make for an easier style of living—doing dishes, answering correspondence, paying bills, and throwing out useless papers. Avoidance of such basic life tasks accumulates your inconveniences and diminishes your chance to enjoy life.

You also inconvenience others by procrastinating. If you turn in a term paper after the term has ended and the professor's vacation has begun, you give him an extra unpleasant task. If you arrive late for an appointment with a collaborator, you may throw her schedule off, particularly if she has another appointment soon after you arrive. Spending excessive time washing up in the community bath basin may delay others. Dawdling in starting on a ski trip may inconvenience prompt companions and result in further delays from longer lift lines and more crowded highways. As a procrastinator, you tend to act so self-absorbedly and oversensitively to yourself that you behave insensitively to others. While you may chastise yourself for this problem, sometimes you may magically believe that others have no reason to hassle you for your tarrying. By this irresponsible behavior, you frequently alienate friends, collaborators, professors, and those whose schedules you help set back. Maude's chronic tardiness heightens the risk that her friends will arrive late for work, and it jeopardizes her friendships.

Situational Procrastination

You may procrastinate over writing a report that has no clear deadline, but demonstrate remarkable efficiency when you have an irrevocable limit. You may act efficiently in answering correspondence on your job but not personal correspondence. Sometimes you may willingly mow the lawn, but balk at sweeping the floor. The locus of your procrastination can vary considerably in terms of the nature of the task.

Priorities and Procrastination

You may have numerous duties which require immediate attention, as meeting a publication deadline, keeping up with work on the job, planning a session for the Elks' annual picnic, shopping for a spouse's birthday present, or studying for a professional examination. You had best make a conscious choice and set priorities as to which project to undertake first, and which second. In such conditions, if you proceed as effectively as you can, you do not procrastinate even if you delay some of your projects.

Even if you set sound priorities and follow through with them, you may still see your actions as procrastination. Regardless of how much work you do, or how efficiently you do it, you may foolishly regard your performance as inadequate. By this foolish and unrealistic definition, you suffer needless mental anguish.

Time Uses and Values

Others may view you as a conspicuous procrastinator, but you may not regard yourself as one. Some individuals just don't view their delays as important, but believe that people in this culture suffer a neurosis about time—trying to jam too much activity into their lives. If your behavior does not impair the functioning of others, and you feel comfortable taking life in a leisurely fashion, what does it matter if you behave less efficiently than others? On the other hand, if you risk losing your job by constantly showing up late for work, why not wisely rethink what you might best do, if you don't want to get fired? In this aspect of your life you may not have much freedom to select your hours, and you may choose to compromise.

Procrastination Variations

Probably no one *always* procrastinates. Maude, who deplores her dallying, rarely emphasizes the many things she does efficiently, including preparing her lesson plans for school, shopping for food and clothing, and paying her rent. While almost everybody procrastinates to some degree, if you characterize yourself as a procrastinator, you neglect looking at your actions as a whole, and falsely label yourself. This reality distortion often leads to a self-fulfilling prophecy.

Joe may rigidly avoid writing letters and bug himself about his pile of correspondence, yet eagerly throw himself into completing the types of administrative detail work that Abigail vigorously resists, and hates herself for avoiding. Both suffer emotional upset, because they think badly of themselves for failing to do the tasks they pick as important. Not only do Joe and Abigail procrastinate in different areas, but the nature of their upsets may differ in kind and intensity. Joe feels guilty about falling behind in his correspondence, and fears he will lose his friends who wait for return letters. Abigail feels depressed because she doesn't get started on her administrative work and views herself as helpless and hopeless. While both persons deprecate themselves, Abigail does so more severely.

Summary

Procrastination means delay—but more than that. It usually stems from and includes several emotional difficulties. For you not only inconvenience yourself and others by resorting to it—but choose *needlessly* and *foolishly* to harm yourself or them.

As we shall show in more detail in the next chapter, you tend to denigrate yourself, act hostilely to your associates, and exhibit low frustration tolerance when you senselessly postpone important projects. Whereupon, viewing yourself as weak and procrastinating, you may down yourself for *that* weakness, then believe yourself incapable of acting better, and drive yourself to further delay.

You can break this vicious neurotic circle through understanding and action. So let us try to help you gather the former, before you send yourself, helter-skelter, into the latter. Later on in this book, we will suggest some ingenious techniques that have helped our clients rid themselves of procrastinating behavior and enjoy more effective and satisfying lives.

2. Main Causes of Procrastination

What we call emotional disturbance seems to arise from three basic causes, which frequently overlap. And procrastination does not appear an exception to this general rule. Let us list these three main factors.

Self-Downing

People mainly (and most often) disturb themselves by putting themselves down—which often leads to anxiety, depression, despair, hopelessness, lack of self-confidence, feelings of worthlessness. These tend to stem from the desire of practically all persons: (1) to perform important tasks adequately; (2) to experience the approval or love of others whom they consider significant; and (3) to escalate these desires into absolutistic, dogmatic, dire necessities. If they would only stick to their desires and not stupidly insist that they *should, ought, must,* and unequivocally *have to* have what they intensely want, they would not get into serious emotional difficulties—though of course they would often feel sad or frustrated when they did not get their wants fulfilled.

But many earthians have little tolerance for merely *wanting* and a high degree of compulsivity toward *needing.* To some degree, they learn necessitizing from their need-oriented parents and culture. "You *must* not steal, dear!" "You *have to* go to school." "You *need to* get along well with others." But even when they don't pick it up this way, they seem to have strong innate tendencies to prefer to *create* and *invent* musts.

Does a child learn or pick up necessities that directly drive it to procrastinate? It wouldn't seem so. It hears, from almost every authoritative and parenting source, exactly the opposite: "You must *not* procrastinate!" "You *have to* get to school on time." "You *should* do your compositions right away!"

But do these kinds of *musts* propel you toward procrastination? Perhaps. For if you *must* not delay things, and you sometimes for various reasons do delay them, you can easily make the obvious conclusion: "Since I did what I *mustn't*, I amount to a no-good person. If I rate as no good, how can I possibly do a good thing, like finishing important tasks early?"

Condemning yourself for procrastinating, in other words, can foster even *more* delay. But this would hardly explain why you started dallying in the first place.

That explanation lies in a more general kind of *must*—that you utterly *have to* perform virtually *all* important tasks adequately and win the approval or love of *every* person you consider significant. This general game of *must*urbation can really cook you to a cinder. Believing this kind of absolutistic rot, you find it necessary to perform innumerable tasks perfectly—such as essays, school tests, sports, social conversation, dancing, and hell knows what else. And if you don't fulfill this "necessity"? Obviously, you sink to total turdhood.

The antidote to this kind of "turdhood"? Oddly enough, many people find it in various kinds of procrastination. For if you *must* do an essay well and you procrastinate long enough in writing it, you will tend to hand it in late (or not at all). Then your poor mark "of course" will stem from your lateness, rather than from your intrinsic inability to write well. And if you *have to* play basketball well, but you show up so late that your team won't let you participate in the game at all, how will anyone ever know that you can't do as well as you *should* do?

Your absolutistic demand (rather than your relativistic desire) to do well at almost anything, then, may impel you to avoid doing that thing on time or to find an excuse for never doing it at all. This demand, and the anxiety to which it almost inevitably leads, will sap your energies, take away your incentive for finishing important tasks, focus your attention on others' opinions rather than on the value of active participation in a project, convince you that no good reason exists for doing many thing, minimize your joy in actively doing something, sidetrack you from gaining skill and ease at performance; and in many other ways sabotage your buckling down to do things.

Overweening anxiety may not serve as the only cause for procrastination. But it certainly helps!

Low Frustration Tolerance

The second main cause of procrastination consists of low frustration tolerance—and, as in the case of overeating, over-indulgence in drugs and alcohol, or avoidance of hard work, you may have this as the primary cause. LFT has an immense effect on human affairs, and RET uniquely stresses its importance. Frequently, it exacerbates and sustains emotional disturbance; just as frequently it seems to directly cause it.

Consider, first, the role of LFT in helping you to maintain self-defeating behavior that you cause yourself with anxiety-provoking *shoulds* and *musts*. You may foolishly tell yourself, "I *have to* get an A—or at the very least a B+ —in English Lit, or I won't have a high enough average to get me into graduate school. Then my life will seem absolutely worthless!" Because you tell yourself this nonsense, you feel afraid to study English Lit to the best of your ability as your final exam approaches. You've then put off reading your textbook and going over your notes. As the days go by, your panic about not getting an A in the course increases; but, perversely enough, you study less and procrastinate more.

Naturally, you tend to loathe your sensations of panic. For who likes to experience butterflies in the stomach, trembling of the limbs, or a rapid pulse? Not you! And you note that, virtually every time you sit down to study, these sensations tend to increase. Coping with the English Lit itself tends to remind you that you may *not* obtain an A or a B+ in the course—and you illogically conclude, when you bring this thought to mind again, "How *awful* if I don't! I couldn't bear ending up with a B—or, worse horrors, a C! That would end my career hopes *forever!*"

In other words, every time you force yourself to study, your fundamental *must* reasserts itself ("I *must* excel in English!"), and this *must* (and not, as you erroneously believe, merely focusing on English Lit itself) brings about increased feelings of panic. You therefore tend to put off studying all the more.

Of equal importance: You realize, since you not only watch what you do (and don't do) but also watch how you think and feel about your actions, that studying—or even contemplating studying—immediately leads to severe anxiety. And you probably realize as well (by prior experience with this sort of thing) that if you force yourself to study, your anxiety will ultimately tend to decrease. For one thing, the studying itself can distract you from your awfulizing by occupying your mind with another kind of subject matter. For another thing, as you study and start learning more and more English Lit, you see that your chance of getting a good mark increases. So, on that count your anxiety will tend to evaporate. You (consciously or unconsciously) conclude, therefore, "I'd better stop the nonsense, no matter how anxious I *now* feel, and settle down to work. *Then* I'll feel much better!"

At this point, however, your low frustration tolerance tends to come into play to sabotage your activity. LFT arises when you recognize that in order to receive *future* gain, you have to undertake *present* pain—see that pain as *awful* and *unbearable* and *too much* to undertake, or even to contemplate. You specifically have the quite reasonable idea (rational Belief), "I find the panic that goes with studying English difficult to bear—I wish I didn't have to feel it and could avoid it," but you also have the unreasonable idea (irrational Belief), "I find it *too* hard to bear. I can't stand it. Even if it may prove only temporary, I *must* avoid it at all costs!"

This philosophy, "I cannot stand present pain for future gain," the central core of LFT, invites you—practically *commands* you—to continue your procrastination about studying English Lit, in light of your belief that such study will set the stage for your severe anxiety about failing. Without the LFT, you might force yourself to study in order to tackle and conquer your anxiety. With it, you will see reviewing English (or at least the panic state that accompanies such reviewing) as a horrible plague—which you will desperately try to avoid.

Almost always, then, when you recognize the value of facing certain unpleasantries, including anxiety, in order to ultimately work through them or get them out of the way, yet you fail to actualize this attitude in order (ultimately) to improve the quality of your life, you nullify what Myles Friedman and George Kelly have called your unique human ability for rationality: your pre diction process. You "know" that if you perform an onerous task, such as studying, you will probably get good results and without it you will tend to obtain undesirable results. But you more vigorously and powerfully "know" that you "can't stand" the *immediate* or *short-term* discomforts of performing the task—the dislike of the task itself or of the anxiety that accompanies it. So you asininely vote in favor of the present "gain"—and the future pain.

As the last sentence shows, LFT not only encourages you to prolong (often indefinitely) some kind of anxiety (or phobia, obsession, or compulsion), but it also constitutes the main and most direct cause of procrastination. For, in the illustration we use here, you probably not only avoid studying English Lit because you tend to make yourself anxious when you *think* of getting less than an A in the course, but because you remind yourself of that anxiety when you contemplate studying. You actually often refuse to study because of your LFT about the pain of studying *itself*. For you will seldom achieve ecstasy when you sit down to read your text or go over your English Lit notes. Instead, you may find that studying: (1) often bores you; (2) requires long hours; (3) keeps you from more enjoyable pursuits (such as socializing or reading light fiction); (4) includes related onerous tasks, such as outlining the material you read or typing your notes; (5) deprives you of rest or sleep; (6) involves your transporting yourself to a suitable work place, such as a study hall or a library; (7) brings about disagreements with friends, relatives, or intimate associates; and (8) involves various other disadvantages.

If you have normal or high frustration tolerance, you take these disadvantages of studying in stride, and sensibly conclude, "Okay, so they exist. I don't like keeping my nose to the grindstone, but who says I have to like it? The studying won't go on forever. And it has some real advantages! Part of it will interest me and I'll probably benefit from some things I learn. Anyway, whether I like it or not, I won't like the disadvantages of *not* studying. For if I fail or get a low mark, I'll have to repeat the damned course later. I could keep myself out of grad school and have a black mark on my record forever! My parents will feel disappointed. My friends won't think much of my abilities. Et cetera!"

Recognizing the hassles of studying, while accurately acknowledging the *greater* disadvantages of procrastinating, you will then probably force yourself back to your books, and you may even partly enjoy doing so. At the very least, your attitude of high frustration tolerance will help you reduce— though not eliminate—your frustrations. For you will get the studying done and view it only as a hassle, not a horror.

Low frustration tolerance, however, leads you to almost opposite conclusions. When you have LFT—or you self-defeatingly convince yourself that you *can't stand* the trouble required to bring about various satisfactions you seek—you inflate an inconvenience into a monster. You start with a value that seems appropriate enough and you empirically observe some of the unpleasant short-run consequences of striving for this value. Thus, you observe that disadvantages truly exist when you actually start to study. You then rationally conclude, "Because I find certain aspects of the study unbeneficial, I do not like these aspects."

Fine—up to this point. But when you abandon these appropriate values, you tend to make what we call, in rational-emotive therapy, a magical jump. You make several more conclusions which involve arrant overgeneralizations, some of which lie entirely outside the realm of empiricism, and which no one can prove or disprove. For example: (1) "Because I don't like some things about studying, I can't enjoy any of it *at all*." (2) "Things I don't like doing should not exist!" (3) "Because I don't like them, I find it *awful* that they exist." (4) "The way I live seems just too hard." (5) "I *can't bear* studying!" (6) "I *deserve* better than this!" (7) "Professors who make me do unfair and difficult tasks rate as *rotten people*." (8) "Because they behave so rottenly, they don't deserve to live and can just drop dead!" (9) "They deserve punishment and damnation." (10) "Because they treat me so unfairly, I won't do what they ask me to do, even if I cut off my nose to spite my face!" (11) "If I don't study, but instead try to get back at them for doing me in, they'll feel sorry and realize they have treated me unjustly." (12) "By rebelling against studying, I'll make things better for myself, and even if I don't, at least I'll help change the world so other students won't have to suffer unfairly in the future." (13) "If I rebel against studying, I'll get a hero's acclaim and show the world what a great person can do!"

When you have LFT, you tend to believe devoutly in hypotheses and conclusions like these—just about none- of which squares with reality and several of which have magical, unprovable (and undisprovable) referents. You state that you cannot enjoy *any* part of studying *at all*, when you probably can enjoy some aspects of it. You claim that you *can't bear* the difficulty of things like studying, when you obviously can—since you probably won't die of studying, and you don't have to feel *entirely* miserable when doing it. You hold that your teachers will feel sorry about forcing you to study, when obviously they won't. You vow you'll make the world better for yourself and others by refusing to do your English Lit, when it seems most unlikely that this outcome will occur.

Anti-empirically, then, your LFT leads you to make statements that just don't accord with reality. It also involves several magical statements: that a law of the universe exists which holds that you must not experience unpleasant things; that when inconveniences do occur in your life, you have to find them *awful*—meaning, at least 101% bad or obnoxious; that some force in the world shows special interest in you and insist that you *deserve* to have things made easy and enjoyable; that people who put difficulties in your way have nothing but rottenness in them and deserve damnation; and that you will gain nobility and sanctification by doing the absolutely right thing of rebelling against studying.

Low frustration tolerance tends to boil down to the proposition, "Things that I consider undesirable (but can't avoid if I'm to get what I want) ought not to exist and I can't stand it if they do!" Reality contradicts this proposition, since things you find undesirable *do* exist and you normally *do* stand them when they exist. When you view an assignment in a realistic manner by observing that it appears inconvenient and unfortunate but will help you achieve a certain goal, you may then complete it with a modicum of delay. When you consider the assignment *absolutely awful* and tell yourself you *can't stand it*, your LFT leads you to feel much more annoyed and frustrated about relatively minor irritations than you otherwise would feel, and you either temporarily put off or entirely avoid dealing with them.

Some form of LFT exists in almost every instance of procrastination and it directly or indirectly contributes to your self-sabotaging delay. Not that everyone with low frustration tolerance procrastinates—some people express it in other ways: as by blowing hassles out of proportion, nonetheless dealing with them, and then whining about having to encounter them. But intolerance of frustration frequently moves people into nonmoving. Whenever you continue to procrastinate, look for this attitude.

In the example we gave earlier, Maude has low frustration tolerance in wanting to meet new men easily, cleaning the dishes without effort, and throwing out newspapers. She recognizes her LFT, and rates herself as a rotten person for having it. She then feels that, because she has intrinsic rottenness, she *can't* do anything, such as clean the dishes, effectively. Here, her low frustration tolerance results in procrastination, her procrastination encourages her to down herself, her self-downing makes her believe she has no ability to stop procrastinating. So, as a result of this vicious cycle, which includes the idea, "Dishwashing makes life too hard, I *can't bear* it," and the idea, "I can't endure my procrastination; I can't accept myself with it, and I can't undo it," she goes 'round and 'round, adding new self-destructive attitudes on each lap of her vicious circle.

You tend to experience LFT that leads to needless delaying and self-downing *about* your procrastinating on several different levels:

Level one: "Cleaning the dishes day after day proves just too hard, and I really can't do them as they accumulate. Things that hard shouldn't bedevil a *schnook* like me!" Result: procrastination.

Level two: "I've put off doing the dishes for a week now and I know I have this horrible weakness, but there seems absolutely nothing I can do about it now. Since I have this atrocious trait and can't give it up, I feel worthless and doomed to have it forever!" Result: more procrastination.

Level three: "Because I have this horrible trait of procrastination, and because even if I thought I could cure it I just wouldn't have the perseverance, I might as well not even work at it. Or maybe I'll try to work on it tomorrow." Result: procrastination about working against procrastination.

On and on goes the joyless merry-go-round!

Hostility

Hostility and low frustration tolerance have a good deal in common.

The first two *musts* with which you create your emotional disturbances consist of, again, (1) "I *have to* do well (sometimes perfectly) to win others' approval," and (2) "The conditions under which I live *must* turn out well (or perfectly well) and give me all the important things I want without any hassles or disadvantages." We now, as another prime cause of problems in general and procrastination in particular, consider (3) "Other people *must* treat me fairly, kindly, and considerately and do what I want." This third dictum results in feelings of anger, resentment, hostility, rage, fury, and sometimes vindictiveness, feuds, and wars.

How does anger contribute to procrastination? In several important ways. For one thing, many of the tasks you accept involve other people. A parent, for example, asks you to do a chore, and you say you will do it. A friend arranges to meet you for dinner and you agree to meet at 6:00 P.M. You decide that you want to get your mate a birthday gift before October 1.

You may delay meeting all these deadlines because, consciously or unconsciously, you feel hostile toward your parent, friend, or mate. If so, you almost certainly have some kind of unreasonable, magical demand that you keep wielding against this individual. Thus, about your parent: "He has *no right* to ask me to lend him a thousand dollars, when he has more money than I have. He *shouldn't* do a thing like that to me—so I won't rush to the bank and arrange to lend him the money, even though I said I would."

About your friend: "A fine friend! The last two times she asked me to go to dinner with her, she stuck me with the check. Whenever I ask other friends to dinner, we take turns paying the check—or at least we split it. But not her! I know she'll try the same thing again tonight. Well, she can't act that way and still call herself my friend. I'll show her! Why should I rush to meet her at six, when she'll treat me so shabbily?"

About your mate: "He'd really like that watch for a gift. I feel sure he would. But what does he ever get me? Nothing worth talking about! When I had a birthday last April, he said he'd get me the jade bracelet I want. That was five months ago! So why should I kill myself trying to get the watch for him?"

Similarly, we may delay doing something because doing it would favor someone else when we don't feel like granting that person a favor. This does not mean that hostility usually or even often leads to procrastination—as some of the psychodynamic therapists, who tend to follow imaginative hypotheses, rather than clinical facts, often claim. Most procrastination probably has little to do with others and much to do with your low frustration tolerance and feelings of inadequacy. But occasionally you may delay important tasks because of your anger toward the people associated with you in the performance of these tasks.

More frequently, you may use hostility as a rationalization for procrastination. Thus, you want to avoid doing a term paper because you fear failing at it, so you put it off to give yourself an alibi for doing it sloppily and inadequately. Then, rather than face your own motives for delay, you either use or invent hostility toward, say, your roommate for making it difficult for you to do the paper, your professor for giving it to you, your parents for sending you to a crummy school that requires term papers, or some other individuals whom you connect with the paper. Instead of feeling hostile toward yourself, you wind up feeling hostile to others for supposedly placing you in an untenable position.

You could also make yourself hostile as a result of your low frustration tolerance. You could view this same onerous term paper as not merely hard but *too* hard for you to work at, and you could wail that the school shouldn't make it that hard for you. As a "logical" next step, you could then hate the school authorities, your professor, and even your fellow students for allowing the school to have so difficult a program, and you could wind up hating the system and the "perpetrators" of the system.

Statistically speaking, your serious procrastinating will more likely relate to your feelings of inadequacy and your LFT than to your feelings of hostility. But the latter may exist as causative factors, too; and occasionally hatred may serve as a primary rather than secondary cause of neurotic delay.

Summary

Three *mus*turbational commandments lie at the core of almost all forms of emotional disturbance: (1) "I must do well!" (2) "You must do well by me!" and (3) "The world must treat me well!" When these *musts* fail to work out, the first leads to anxiety, depression, and self-downing; the second to anger, hostility, and resentment; and the third to depression and hopelessness, accompanying an attitude of low frustration tolerance.

In regard to procrastination, the most frequent command states: "The world must give me the things I want without my expending any great effort or suffering deprivation. Until it does, I'll put off future gain for present ease." The next common imperative: "I must have outstanding accomplishments and acclaim. And if I don't have such guarantees, I might as well put off tough jobs." The third insistence: "You must treat me fairly and kindly. And if you don't, I'll spite you by goofing, even though I may cut off my nose in the process!"

These three self-defeating philosophies, which we easily tend to invent and which our cultures often foster, don't guarantee that we will procrastinate. But they certainly heighten the chance that we will!

3. A Rational Approach to Overcoming Procrastination

People live in three main ways: cognitively, emotively, and behaviorally. And they do so interactively or transactionally. Their thinking inextricably intertwines with their emoting and their behaving, so that they rarely think, emote, or act in a *pure* way. When, for example, you watch television instead of doing your school work, you *act* inefficiently. But while you move or behave in this manner, you think about what you do ("I don't have to study right now, I can do it tomorrow. I'll enjoy myself more if I watch television tonight"). Simultaneously you have affects about what you do—such as feeling pleased about watching the television and guilty about not doing your homework.

To change a behavior pattern, therefore, you usually have to (1) act differently about it, (2) think in some manner other than the way you have thought about it up to now, and (3) have pronounced feelings or affects about changing it. Ideally, if you work hard at all of these—at acting, thinking, and feeling differently about the pattern you want to modify—you will tend to change it more quickly, completely, and enduringly than if you mainly emphasize only one of these behaviors. Consequently efficient forms of therapy, like rational-emotive therapy, try to get you to do, and to keep forcefully doing, all three of these things—acting, thinking, and feeling in such a manner as to push yourself toward change and also stopping yourself from falling back, later, to the original undesired behavior.

So with procrastination. We shall show you various behavioral, cognitive, and emotive ways of working against it. We start here with some of the main cognitive or rational ways, since the system we practice as psychotherapists, rational-emotive therapy, notably and almost uniquely stresses these ways. I (A.E.) developed this system a number of years ago and have written extensively about it, as shown in the references listed in the back of this book; and we continue to teach it and use it for many kinds of emotional problems at the Institute for Advanced Study in Rational Psychotherapy in New York and at allied institutes throughout the world. I (W.K.) have specialized in applying it to procrastination difficulties and with children.

In this chapter we shall outline some of the RET principles and practices that you can use in helping yourself overcome needless delay. We start with the cognitive methods. because they play an unusually important part in originating, maintaining, and finally minimizing all kinds of emotional problems; and because you probably can better understand the behavioral and emotive techniques we later outline, if you have a good cognitive background.

The ABC's of RET

A central theory of the RET cognitive-behavioral approach: "You feel the way you think." We can illustrate this with the ABC's of RET. When you have either an appropriate or inappropriate emotional reaction or consequence (C) to some Activating Experience or Activating Event (A), the Activating Event alone doesn't cause your emotional Consequence. Instead, your Belief system (B) spurs you to react emotionally at C and, often, to act on your emotions.

In other words, your Belief system (thoughts, attitudes, values) stimulates your feelings and your actions. You direct your actions by your thoughts.

A novel idea? Hardly! Over two thousand years ago, Epictetus and his student Marcus Aurelius propounded this viewpoint. Later philosophers, such as Immanuel Kant and Bertrand Russell, recognized the prepotency of thinking in generating feelings and actions. Many psychologists, such as Alfred Adler, Jean Piaget, Magda Arnold, Stanley Schacter, and Richard Lazarus, have emphasized the validity of this concept. Thus the pioneering work of Ellis, in developing a cognitive-emotive therapeutic system has much philosophical and empirical support. Recent studies by DiLoreto, Meichenbaum and Goodman, Goldfried and his associates, Trexler, Velten, and many others have supported its effectiveness as a behavioral change system.

The Goals and Values of the System

Each psychotherapy or self-help system has its implicit or explicit goals. Rational-emotive therapy falls into the second class. RET values survival and satisfaction in living, including doing what we reasonably can to help the human race survive, getting along with members of the social group or community, relating intimately with a few selected members of that group, enjoying productive work, and self-acceptance. Although we cannot absolutely prove these goals as good, few would dispute them. Once we choose them, we can define rationality as any behavior or thought which furthers such goals. We can also deem irrational any thinking or action which interferes with the attainment of those goals.

The Two Faces of B

We identify irrational Beliefs (iB's) as beliefs which stimulate over-reactions, such as anxiety, depression, rage, or under-reactions, such as apathy and inertia. We identify rational Beliefs (rB's) as those which hold together logically and result in appropriate emotional and behavioral reactions that further basic goals. Each person, at any one time, may think alternately in both ways, with one belief system dominating, or each balancing the other. Rational-emotive therapy provides a method of identifying and diminishing the irrational elements in personal belief systems. However, prior to demonstrating how to accomplish this, let us look at how much impact belief systems and interpretations of events can have on feelings and behavior.

The Potency of a Belief

The Hindu religion endorses a belief in the process of reincarnation, wherein all creatures get reborn and come back at a higher level in the animal kingdom, provided they behaved as best they could in their former lives. Thus, you may move up from existence as a worm, and enter into your next life as a dog. In fact, you can keep going up the scale until you reach the level of a human. Once human, you would start from the lowest order, the untouchables, and end with the highest order, the Brahmans, or priests. As an untouchable, you would remain in a quasi-slave caste and do all the work that an upper-class Indian wouldn't think of doing, such as handling dead bodies, cleaning your house, or performing other activities thought of as "unclean."

Your belief in perfect servitude as a way to get reborn into a higher caste in the next life would assert a powerful influence. Thus, for centuries few untouchables rebelled. To rebel would have risked a return to a lower level of life or a rebirth into the same caste system. Also, you would have rebelled against "better people" who had already evolved to their current status through their perfection in lower stations. You can see why Hindu beliefs in reincarnation prevailed for centuries!

But Westerners have their crazy beliefs too! Our forefathers, in Salem, Massachusetts, drowned some women or burned them at the stake because they thought they were witches and held them responsible for crop failures and pestilence. This belief in witches created terror among the American settlers, and simultaneously a sense of Jehovian justice, which they believed sanctified killing certain unusual individuals. Thus, belief led to self-terrorizing as well as witch-hunting.

Believing the earth flat guided the behavior of twelfth- and thirteenth-century people until Columbus confirmed the theory of Copernicus that the world was round. In earlier times, most sailors would not venture out of sight of shore for fear of falling over the edge of the earth, and facing ferocious beasts waiting with open jaws and flashing teeth.

In the above examples, people strongly tend to treat their beliefs as unassailable truths. If you identify what you believe with fact (belief equals fact), then you prime yourself to think in absolutistic terms and to guide your feelings and actions accordingly. When you base your beliefs on unobjective and nonverifiable myths, you can create unnecessary troubles.

To show how the manner in which you interpret significantly affects your feelings and actions, consider the following examples:

You can identify a long narrow object in the woodlands either as a stick or a snake. Your interpretation has considerable importance. Suppose you view it as a rattlesnake? Will you *run*!

You, a policeman, chase a fleeing robber, order him to halt, and see him slow down and begin to turn around. Does he turn around to surrender, or does he turn to fire a gun?

Your split-second judgment may mean your life, the robber's, neither, or both. Your *expectation* has prime importance. If you expect the robber to turn around with a pipe in his hand, you likely won't fire. If you expect him to have a gun and he turns around holding the corncob pipe he likes to smoke, he may never see the light of dawn.

The way you evaluate yourself often forms the basis for your emotive-behavioral reaction. Thus, if you define yourself as weak and ineffectual, you may so envelop yourself in this self-perception of incapability that you fritter away time worrying and consequently procrastinate. You, like the Hindus, ancient sailors, and the Salem witch hunters, may operate in an all-or-none fashion and never think to verify the hypothesis from which you generate your actions.

Using RET, we can examine this process of treating beliefs as though 100% correct, and identify and change our false beliefs and erroneous assumptions.

The ABC's at Work

Rational-emotive therapy provides a structured method to examine, then minimize or eliminate, maladaptive beliefs which interfere with effective functioning, promote procrastination, and block you from achieving basic goals of survival, satisfaction, affiliation, and intimacy. It provides the tools and rationale for you to develop a philosophy and skills to achieve the life style you desire.

The method works as follows: First, identify the Activating Event about which you procrastinate (A). Second, identify the emotional Consequences you experience while procrastinating (C). Third, identify your accompanying Beliefs and self-statements (B). Fourth, identify your behavioral Reaction of procrastinating and avoiding (R). Finally, you can objectively view your problem and dispute your irrational Beliefs (iB's) until you become able to effect changes in your procrastinating behavior.

Consider Debbie's problem of doing the dishes:

Activating Event—observing dirty dishes in the sink.
Beliefs—"How annoying to clean them, but I'd better." (rational)
   —"I can't stand this mess. It looks too tough to tackle." (irrational)

Consequence—frustration. (rational)
  —anxiety, "unbearable" frustration. (irrational)
Reaction—do the dishes. (rational)
                    or
          avoid washing the dishes. (irrational)

Assuming that your irrational Belief dominated, you would predominantly feel anxiety and "unbearable" frustration and you would probably try to avoid this anxiety and frustration rather than eliminate your Belief. If your rational Belief dominated, and you mainly felt the appropriate emotion of real frustration at rC (rational Consequence), you would tend to do the dishes. You would do so to reduce your frustration and thereby gain greater satisfaction. If you didn't do so, you might also have secondary irrational ideas stimulated from your primary irrational emotive consequences and your observation that the dirty dishes remain undone. The General Semanticists call these second-order problems.

Thus, instead of doing the dishes, you may avoid facing the problem by overeating or calling friends on the telephone or watching television. Feeling overwhelmed with self-hate, you may irrationally pity yourself and bemoan your ineptitude. You may then cancel out on a party, or fail to begin a report, or resort to other irrational reactions.

Or you may start a semipositive behavioral reaction. To avoid thinking about the dirty dishes, you may complete other projects you procrastinated about. You may write a term paper or pay your overdue telephone bill, and this serves as a tolerable diversion.

The behavioral reactions of avoidance and diversion can alert you that you have resorted to irrational thinking.

Tipping the Balance by Disputing Irrationality

You can tip your irrationality-rationality balance in favor of the rational system of thinking and acting by identifying and disputing irrational self-assumptions and subjecting them to a logico-empirical analysis. Armed with an arsenal of rational questions, you can make yourself aware of the illogical dimensions of your problem, rigorously examine faulty basic assumptions, and shatter the very foundations of your irrational Belief system.

Two outlines of the irrational chain leading to procrastination illustrate how Disputing works. Let us first see how Debbie rationally attacked her problem. Debbie asked herself, "What 'it' do I think I can't stand?" Her answer: "My anxiety about not washing the dishes." She quickly recognized that, since she had felt anxious for several weeks, she *had* stood her anxiety—although she clearly had not liked either viewing the unwashed dishes or her tendency to avoid doing them. She also asked herself, "How have I gone out of control?" and saw "out of control" as a higher-order abstraction. She realized that, concretely, she only failed to control a small segment of her behavior—washing the dishes—some of the time. So she didn't *really* act "out of control" and didn't have to awfulize about this "loss."

After ridding herself of anxiety and self-downing about procrastinating, Debbie saw that the procrastination itself stemmed from the irrational Beliefs that dishwashing proved *too* hard and that she *shouldn't* have to do it. She thought she should feel *naturally* motivated.

When asked why she had to feel naturally motivated to do the dishes, she couldn't think of any reasons except that she couldn't stand frustrating things like washing the dishes. She next looked at the question for the second time, and asked herself, "What makes frustration so terrible?" she replied, "After all, I stand the frustration of watching the dishes pile up. And *that* doesn't seem awful. So why must I think it *awful* to work at eliminating this frustration by *doing* the dishes?"

By examining her irrational Beliefs, Debbie saw that she didn't have to feel happy about doing the dishes in order to do them, that she could stand both the dishwashing and her anxiety about not doing it. She also pushed herself to do the dishes, and found the task less irksome than she previously had thought. This combination of working against her irrational thinking patterns and alleviating the problem through activity resulted in a new cognitive, emotive, and behavioral effect. She began to appraise the task rationally as mildly frustrating and to enjoy getting it done, if not the actual doing.

Paul's domestic problem provides a second illustration of how to identify and dispute irrational premises. After months of listening to his wife put him down for not quickly moving up the corporate ladder, Paul began to question why he procrastinated about asserting his dislike for her behavior. He traced part of his reluctance to fear that she would criticize him even more and that he couldn't stand such criticism.

Also: fear that she might consider him a weakling if he didn't act firmly with her. Moreover, despite their poor relationship over the years, he felt deathly afraid of living alone should she decide to leave him—and imagined himself lonely and unwanted in his old age. As he thought about these fears, he began to see that he had built a monster in his mind, much like the sailors of olden times had done when they feared dropping off the face of the earth.

He asked himself: "What evidence have I that my wife will think me weak if I stand up to her? How do I know she'll leave me? And if she did, would that prove *awful*?" He could see that his worst premonitions probably would *not* materialize. And even if his wife left him, he wouldn't *have* to spend the rest of his life in solitude. Further, since he had tied his procrastination about asserting himself to his personal inadequacy, by questioning how his wife's leaving him would diminsh his value as a total human, he could see that it would only if he *thought* it would! He concluded that he felt inferior when his wife tried to put him down, because he *concurred* with her view of him. He also realized that, if worse came to worse and his wife left him, he might initially have a difficult time making new contacts but that he could, through persistence, meet many new women and find a more interesting and tolerant partner.

Paul decided to stop procrastinating and to speak to his wife about her putting him down. He picked a calm moment and diplomatically tried to explain how he felt about their relationship. His wife began to scream and insisted that he had to succeed on the job, because she constantly felt embarrassed by his low corporate position. He then tried to get her into marital counseling. She refused. He separated from her. At that point she agreed to work on her emotional over-reactions, and Paul said he would try again, but only if they both went for counseling.

As a consequence of this experience, Paul reported that he felt positive about asserting himself. Through the process of confronting his wife, he found that he gained more confidence, that he no longer felt intimidated by her rage, that he could face the realization that the marriage just might not work out, and that assertive action on his part could improve his chances for a better life.

Both Debbie and Paul disputed the irrational assumptions responsible for their anxiety and low frustration tolerance and also actively tried new behaviors to modify their situations and help create new cognitive-emotive-behavioral effects. They used the rational-emotive model to overcome serious procrastination problems.

Disputing Demandingness

Irrational thinking includes a group of demand terms which underlie the two examples just given. For instance: *should, ought, must, expect, have to, got to, need, necessary, require, imperative* and *demand*. While you can rationally assert, "I would find it better if I got this or didn't get that," your demands that you *must* get this or not get that reflect an absolutistic and rigid set of beliefs comparable to the unbending view that many had for centuries about the flatness of the world. Used in the absolutistic sense, either you, someone else, or the universe *has to* act the way you want. For example, "You should feel grateful for all I've done for you" really means, "You must do what I consider right, and you'll look to me like a worthless ingrate, whom I can't stand, if you don't!" Neither of these statements makes sense because (1) they represent a dictatorial attitude which you impose on another; (2) they reduce the possibilities of greater affiliation and intimacy with this other; (3) they result in emotional pain, especially anger.

When rational, you tend to think in *desire* terms: you wish, want, prefer, aspire, hope, trust. These probabilistic terms imply that you anticipate some uncertainty but you clearly prefer attaining something and experience a sense of concern regarding it. Desires reflect a mental attitude of acceptance of reality but not of passive acceptance of *anything* that exists. Indeed, if you desire, you have an increased likelihood of getting what you want, as you don't waste time and energy whining about injustice when you don't get what you believe you absolutely must.

At times you may *use* desire terms but *mean* demands. You can say, "I wish you would stop behaving that way" and really mean, "You *should* stop!" Here your *intent* reflects absolutism although the terms you use do not. How can you discriminate between desire and demandingness? By seeing whether you act overemotionally or overconstrictedly. If you do, you tend to think absolutistically. *Musts* make for misery. *Terrible-izing* makes for anxiety and despair.

You can dispute demandingness and its accompanying inappropriate emotions through self-questioning procedures.

You can examine the statement, "You should feel grateful for all I've done for you. You act like a worthless ingrate when you don't do what I consider right! I can't stand you!" by asking: (1) "What law says a person *should* act differently from the way he or she does act? (2) How can any person rate as totally worthless? (3) Why can't I *stand* what I don't like?" While you may not like another's behavior and can actively try to change it, no rule exists that says humans should not act in "wrong" or "ungrateful" ways. Indeed, no law in the universe dictates that you *should not* act in a procrastinating fashion, although you can find many good reasons why you'd better not.

In the process of challenging or disputing, you often will find yourself bogged down because you wrongly believe that because it might prove better or more advantageous to procrastinate less, you *should not* procrastinate. This doesn't follow! Because you might better do something, it doesn't follow that you have to do it. Sure it would prove better to do what you perceive as more effective! But *desirable* does not equal *should*. Not when you think clearly!

Adrenalin Reduction

A considerable period may elapse between the time you develop a rational view and the moment your body divests itself of excessive adrenalin and other physical results of intense emotion. Irrational thinking creates considerable emotional arousal sometimes, including the secretion of adrenalin, and your system doesn't always immediately recover from that agitation. Rather than giving yourself a secondary problem—that of believing you have failed because you see no immediate diminution of bodily tension—you'd better wait a few minutes to see if your physical reactions don't change in harmony with your acquiring a more rational philosophy. If not, then back to the drawing board!

Effort and Change

Ironically, you may have considerable difficulty conquering procrastination by following the methods outlined in this book for the same reason you probably started procrastinating in the first place: your intolerance of work and effort. For, as we noted earlier, low frustration tolerance remains one of the prime causes of self-defeating lateness. And effort, which usually goes along with reasonably *high* frustration tolerance, serves as the main antidote to almost any emotional problem, including procrastination.

What a double bind! You procrastinate because you think it too hard to get yourself moving to do what you have promised yourself to do. Now you ask us how to stop procrastinating and we sagely say, "By effort. By hard work at thinking, feeling, and behaving differently." "Well," you irritatedly ask, "Don't you mean, then, that I have to pull myself up by my own bootstraps?—work at my nonworkingness?"

Yes, we do mean that. But fortunately we can show you *how* you can do so—by doing some cognitive restructuring. For here we have one of the beauties of rational therapy: It provides strategies for almost every kind of human disturbance, and it includes persuading you, or getting you to persuade yourself, to apply some of these strategies.

The persuasive quality in this particular instance involves your showing yourself, with logic and with facts, that your anti-effort philosophy hardly ever brings about the results—including the lack of effort!—that you try to obtain with it. For, in terms of your original procrastination, you first tell yourself logically, "It seems hard to buckle down to my term paper right now. How much more I'd enjoy going out on a date instead!"

Correct! Dating usually gives more immediate pleasure than writing a term paper. So, if you only care for short-run gains, you may as well go on the date and put off doing the term paper.

But alas! you have other, longer-run profits and losses in life. And, using your head, you can cognitively see and understand that, "Yes, dating seems easier and more desirable *right now*, as I think of sitting down and doing the term paper, but in the *long run* it may prove *much harder*. For the time will soon come when I cannot do the paper before its due date, or when it will require more stress and strain to finish than it would require right now, or when it won't get done at all. And the results—including the fact that some of the most desirable people may refuse to date me or that I won't remain around this university at all and have other students to date—would seem much more disadvantageous than doing the paper right now."

In terms of difficulty, then, which *really* proves harder—

doing the paper right now and taking the consequences of having the date right now and taking its consequences?

Your low frustration tolerance, in other words, stems from your absurd *idea* of what the world has—and should have—in store for you. It does not stem from the *situation* of your having a paper to do or a date to enjoy. And, although you may not fully control these situations, you do control your own ideas!

The same logic applies to the work and effort of overcoming procrastination. You may say to yourself, "I don't like to have to stop procrastinating by *working* at doing so (and, especially, by working at doing so *promptly*). I wish another, easier way existed." A very sensible, same set of evaluations! But you can add to it this insane set: "I hate the work I have to do to stop procrastinating! I *must* find an easier way!" This second set of beliefs—irrational beliefs, of course—will tend to add to, and decidedly not help you overcome, your delaying.

All progress hardly stops, however. Rationally, you can block this nonsense by empirically and logically realizing: "So I don't like to stop my procrastinating by working at doing so. Tough! But I will like *not* working at it even less because then the procrastination, and all its miserable results, will continue. How lovely if an easier way existed? But it doesn't. And I don't *have to* find one. Although both procrastinating and stopping procrastinating seem hard, I have no reason to believe them *too* hard. I'll have a hell of a lot harder time of it if I don't work at stopping!"

In other words, if you don't make a real effort to work against procrastination, you will continue this pernicious habit—and will procrastinate about stopping procrastination! Your two main choices then consist of (1) suffering with the problem forever or (2) continuing to work at it. A grim choice, perhaps. But the second one, for all its difficulty, at least leaves you with less needless delay, many direct and indirect benefits from your newfound promptness, and less emotional anguish. Does the better choice really seem *that* hard to take?

Summary

The rational-emotive method of therapy, which you can apply to yourself whether or not you actually see a therapist, involves the following process:

IDENTIFY (1) your ACTIVATING EVENTS or ACTI-
VATING EXPERIENCES (A); (2) your rational BELIEFS
(rB) and irrational BELIEFS (iB) about those events or experiences; (3) your emotional CONSEQUENCES (C) of
these BELIEFS (B); and (4) your behavioral REACTIONS
(R) that accompany your emotional CONSEQUENCES
(C).

THEN proceed to DISPUTE (D) your irrational BE-
LIEFS (iB's)

UNTIL YOU BRING ABOUT a new cognitive-emotive-
behavioral EFFECT (E)

If you will continually go through the A-B-C-D-E's of
RET whenever you procrastinate (or consider procrastinating), you will tend to wind up with a new EFFECT (E),
which ultimately includes the general idea:

"I wish I could put off this project and not suffer harsh
results. But it doesn't look like I can! I find it distasteful to
get to work on it and finish it promptly. But I'll find it harder
if I don't. I'd better not tell myself that people and conditions
should or *must* not require me to complete this project in
good time when they actually do require it. Too bad! If
things exist this way, I can bear it without liking it and get
what I want in life with minimal discomfort instead of esca-
lating it by needless and self-defeating procrastination. In my
own best interest, I shall keep making a determined effort,
stubbornly refusing to procrastinate about important projects.
If I fail at some of them, tough. If I don't try them at all, a
lot tougher!"

4. Overcoming Procrastination Resulting from Self-Downing

As we have noted in Chapter 2, you often may procrastinate because you feel inadequate and believe that you will prove yourself even more unworthy if you do what you have promised yourself to do—and do it badly. RET and other systems of psychotherapy concentrate on this aspect of disturbance—since it occurs quite frequently and brings about deadly results.

As a hostile person, you will fail to get along very well with others, and to some degree will defeat your most desired goals and values. As a person with low frustration tolerance, you frequently will act like a baby, whine about the conditions under which you live, and usually increase the very annoyances that you wail about. In both instances, you tend to sabotage your best interests.

As a self-downer, you wreak even more damage on your aspirations. For just as soon as you start to denigrate your *self*, your *essence*, your *totality*, you begin to subscribe heavily to the philosophy, "Not only do my performances stink, but *I* stink!" And, as a "stinker" or "worthless person," you see yourself as an individual who (1) hasn't yet performed adequately in a certain area (such as academic achievement), (2) *never can* perform adequately, (3) has hopeless deficiencies in many other important areas, (4) consequently doesn't *deserve* future success or acceptance by others, and (5) will inevitably lose out on "real" happiness for the rest of your life. Such a self-appraisal discourages you from ever trying to change your performances, and leads to anxiety, depression, despair, and hopelessness.

In regard to procrastination, you may tend to feel even more hopeless and worthless—if anyone can feel "more" worthless!—than in regard to other kinds of performances. For don't forget that when you fail at, say, math or English, you may acknowledge that you merely have little talent in those areas, and that no reasonable amount of effort can make up for that lack. So you may regret your deficiency (as you might feel sorry about having a short leg or a crooked nose) but accept yourself *with* it.

Not so with procrastination! For you almost always realize, at least in the beginning, that you consciously *choose* to give in to delaying tactics, that you *could* do otherwise, and that you simply *refuse* to change your ways. Even if you think you have an innate tendency toward laziness, you realize that you have the ability to overcome it—and that you just won't use that ability. You rarely think you *have* to procrastinate; and you therefore tend to down yourself, after you delay long enough, for doing what you don't have to do.

Again, as we showed earlier, no matter how much you rationalize about your procrastination, and make up fancy excuses for not getting your projects done, you usually realize that you have very poor reasons for putting things off or that many of your "reasons" don't hold water. If you fail at something like history, you may have some valid excuses: You have a poor memory, your professor unrealistically gives the class too much work to do, he or she teaches badly, you have too many other things to do this term, or health problems have interfered with your concentration on the subject. But when you see yourself as procrastinating, you normally mean that you *do* have the time and energies to get to your work, but that you rebelliously and foolishly refrain from doing so. Almost by definition, *you* make yourself put things off, and *you* have full responsibility for this laxity.

Consequently you tend to condemn yourself more for your procrastination than you do for your other deficiencies. You also immerse yourself in self-denigrating, circular thinking. You feel unable to do something well (or well enough) and therefore feel unworthy. To keep your "unworthiness" from continually assailing you, you procrastinate at performing this task. You then see that your needless delay has *extra* disadvantages and *itself* constitutes an inadequacy. You then use your procrastination as "proof" of your originally hypothesized "unworthiness."

The problem of self-image constitutes one of the largest and most important areas of personality and seems central to emotional health and disturbance. You base your self-concept on a rating system: (1) on your rating of your traits, deeds, and performances, especially as others view them and rate them; and (2) on your rating of your *self*, your central *core*, your *totality*. When you rate your traits highly, you have what we call in RET achievement-confidence or love-confidence. You know, usually from the results of your past performances, that you do well in various areas and that others will approve of your performances (and, by extension, approve of you for doing them); and you conclude, "Since I have done math well in the past, I have confidence in my ability to do it well in the present and future." And: "Since others have found me competent and liked me in the past, I have a high degree of confidence (I make a firm prediction) that they will find my work good and approve of me today and tomorrow."

This kind of thinking works out fine, for it informs you about what you probably can achieve and about how much approval you likely will get from others for achieving. Achievement-confidence (or work-confidence) and love-confidence (or approval-confidence) help you perform better and get along well with others. If you do not rate your characteristics and performances in this way, you probably will interfere with your basic values of surviving and achieving happiness.

Unfortunately, because you belong to the human race and get reared and educated by other humans (particularly by your parents, but also by your teachers, friends, and mass communicators), you naturally and easily jump from achievement-confidence and love-confidence to self-confidence. You almost always—and quite falsely—conclude, "Because others find me competent and like me, I can see myself as a *good person*, who *deserves* to keep performing well and winning approval." You then have what we usually call "ego strength," "self-esteem," or "self-worth."

But not unconditional self-acceptance! For the fine "ego" that you acquire by rating yourself as a "worthwhile person" for performing well and winning approval really depends on your *continuing* to do so. Obviously, if *you* rate as "good" today, for getting the highest mark in your math class and winning the plaudits of your professor and fellow students, *you* turn into a "bad" or "inadequate" person tomorrow if you do poorly in math—or even get the second highest mark in the class.

Moreover, if your performance or achievement-confidence depends on your doing well, and you want to get good results by acting adequately and by knowing that you probably can do so again in the future, you have a powerful motive or incentive to keep working at math or other subjects. For whatever you *want*, you generally work at achieving. But if your view of *yourself*, your *totality*, your worth *as a person* depends on your accomplishment, you almost always will think you *have to*, or *need to* do well—since the stakes now emerge as enormously important or sacred—and you will then tend (1) to strive *desperately* to accomplish, (2) to feel exceptionally *anxious* or *over*concerned about accomplishing, (3) to focus on your self-image rather than on performing better, and (4) to down your entire self and consider your existence unworthy if you think it likely that you will fail to perform outstandingly.

Because humans, including you, find it so easy to jump magically from rating their *behaviors* to rating their *selves*, and because this kind of self-rating does enormous harm and leads to procrastination and to self-condemnation about procrastinating, we focus in this chapter on rational-emotive techniques of self-acceptance. Such techniques represent methods of accepting your aliveness, your existence, and your you-ness *whether or not* you do well and *whether or not* others wholly approve of you.

How can you acquire skill in eliminating self-ratings while still rating your behaviors and performances? Let us illustrate.

Inferiority Feelings: Case Examples

Roger's boss called him into his office and asked him to supervise a special task force to implement the new self-help program that he had helped develop. Roger thought about it, began to worry that he wouldn't do well, and, fearing he would fail, turned down the position.

Roger clearly qualified for the coveted job. He had the academic background, experience, and knowledge it required. Yet he viewed himself as incompetent and opted to stay at his old desk job, filling out reports, and daydreaming about doing great things. Sure, he would have liked to take the new job, but he made his fear of failure and leaving in "disgrace" the decisive factors in his decision.

Rudy observed a charming woman standing by the window at a cocktail party. He thought how much he would like to meet her, but panicked as he speculated that she would snub him if he tried to start a conversation with her. He ruminated about what he could say, finally decided to force himself to approach her, then noticed her talking to another woman.

Fearing that he would appear impolite if he interrupted them, he decided to wait until the other woman left, and felt relieved that he had a "stay of execution."

Rudy believes he has nothing interesting to say, so he stalls to the point that the women he wants to meet get approached by other men, or go away. His procrastination in approaching members of the other sex closely ties into his perception of himself as inadequate, and his belief that rejection verifies his worthlessness.

Roger and Rudy procrastinate because they believe themselves inferior and unworthy. This problem enters into many avenues of their lives. For example, Rudy would like to ask his physics professor questions, but fears doing so. When he gets up the "courage," he thinks it "too late" to ask—the professor has proceeded to a different topic. He operates much as he did when he considered approaching the woman at the cocktail party.

Roger plays chess well and would like to enter chess tournaments. But he conveniently "forgets" about registering until the deadline has passed. Both Rudy and Roger have considerable anxiety over their projected performance and almost always avoid situations where they may fail.

Much of the lack of confidence exhibited by Roger and Rudy, including the deprivations they thereby impose upon themselves, reflects their view that their intrinsic human value depends upon their actions. Rudy invests success in meeting a woman with his total essence. Then he procrastinates, fearing verification of his "worthlessness." "Oh, how awful," he thinks, "if someone saw me walk over to the girl and heard me stumble over my words. They'd think me an ass to approach this charming female!" His fearful fantasy, leaping over all logic, settles upon the possibility that all women he might approach would see him as a loser and would reject him with expressions of disgust. This line of thinking parallels his procrastination.

Fear of failure includes a cognitive-emotional freezing experience where, when anxiety-riddled, you down yourself in expectation of not living up to your standards.

Personal Worth and Performance: Do They Differ?

In the poem, *Casey at the Bat*, the hero had three swings at the ball before he struck out and went down in infamy for failing to save his team from defeat. Does this episode in

Casey's life render him a person without worth? If a woman of Rudy's choice turns him down, does this render him a valueless person? If Roger performs poorly on his job, does this make him an inferior individual?

This section provides you with a rational-emotive frame of reference for answering these questions.

Your value system gives you a framework for judging worth. For example, if you value national defense, you will tend to support efforts to bolster your nation's armed forces. If you esteem honesty, you will tend to seek out people you view as possessing that quality. We generally select our friends from those to whom we can best relate and who exhibit the morality we espouse. We tend to reject those who display qualities and characteristics that go against our value system.

Humans possess many traits and characteristics valued by some individuals and detested by others. These traits include playfulness, sobriety, exhibitionism, quietness, openness, closedness, etc., which occur in various combinations and allow for many variations. Some traits appear dominating and distinguishing, so that we may acclaim a person for a robust love of life (as Zorba the Greek), or for his inquisitiveness and inventiveness (as Thomas Edison). We may call such traits cardinal traits.

We can view the same trait negatively, positively, or neutrally. A person who suffers from shyness may view a talkative individual as having a desirable trait and an attention-getting person may view this same individual as insensitive and compulsive. The trait of loquaciousness remains stable, but evaluations vary depending upon the listener's frame of reference. Humans frequently define others on the basis of a single trait, and neglect all their other qualities. Indeed, just as people may appreciate a work of art in different ways so they may differently rate other persons. Thus, Sam may want to introduce his friend, Walter, to another friend, Derrick, convinced that they will get on well since each has a good sense of humor, a quality that Sam highly values. But Walter and Derrick actually do not and may never like each other. Walter perceives Derrick as slick and Derrick perceives Walter as frivolous.

We may evaluate thoughts and actions according to various criteria. Since over a lifetime each of us engages in billions of thoughts and actions, we make little effort to examine and rate each one. Moreover, ratings of traits differ according to our differing frames of references. Viewed in the context of industrialized society, we may esteem an American's competitiveness. But some other cultures would deem his competitiveness an unworthy behavior. In certain Polynesian islands, the tribal chief marries the heaviest women. Some even stay in pens, fattening up on tapioca root until he considers them fat enough. Not so in the United States and most European countries! There, people value slimness and shun the obese.

In cultures regulated by laws of supply and demand, some desirable products bring a premium price because of their scarcity. Humans who show desirable traits or talents may likewise command a premium.

Clearly, you may yourself value or devalue your deeds and traits. Because of your ability to generalize (focus upon only one or a few traits and categorize the whole on that basis) you can easily leap from evaluating the worth of your act to evaluating your "total" worth. A teen-age girl who looks tenderly at the leader of the rock band sees only what she wants to see in him. She doesn't see that his private life may vastly differ from what she imagines but views him as the image of perfection—as good a *person*, as she finds his *music*. The man who holds up a grocery store may appear very differently to different eyes—as a beast to the owner of the store, as a victim of poverty to his lawyer, and as a loving son to his mother.

The natural human tendency to generalize has numerous advantages. You need not relearn that you can sit comfortably on certain objects with a particular contour or that you would best avoid *any* large fast-moving object heading directly toward you. You have a natural bent for comparison and discrimination, and these processes provide you with certain life-saving impulses. Recognizing the distinction between the uniforms of friends and enemies during wartime has obvious advantages. Telling the difference between a rattlesnake and a garter snake helps you decide what to do when faced with a long slender moving creature heading toward you in the woods.

We use language for describing generalizations and discriminations, but we tend to make it more encompassing than the things and traits we label. Thus, you may point to an object and call it "a chair" or to a person and call him "Uncle Jim." This labeling process reflects a type of semantic shorthand which helps communication, but can easily lead to overgeneralizations and discrimination deficiencies. In cases where you fail to discriminate between one of your traits or actions and your total essence, and where you overgeneralize about your *self* based upon that lack of discrimination, you can easily set the stage for evaluating this *self* over-positively or over-negatively.

When you perform poorly on an examination you may put yourself down by thinking, "I seem stupid and worthless. I deserve to fail." You then wrongly overgeneralize about yourself on the basis of having done poorly on the test, and forget about your thousands of other actions, traits, and characteristics.

When you neglect to discriminate between your worth as a person and the value (or enjoyability) of your performance, you think perfectionistically and unscientifically. For if you rate *yourself* or *totality* at all (which you really need *not* do), you'd better see yourself as "worthwhile" because you remain alive, rather than because you have done positive deeds. More elegantly, you can see yourself as having an "identity" (uniqueness and ongoingness) but not as having an "ego" (self-rating). You then only evaluate your *acts* (as enjoyable or defeating), but not *yourself* or your *totality*. You do not affix a label to your "essence." Thus Casey need not devalue himself because of the strike-out, as that act does not represent his totality or *self*.

Elaborations on a Definition of Worth

Your concept of personal worth helps or sabotages your joy in living. If you have a sensible view of your "value," you can challenge irrational thinking that leads to self-devaluation, anxiety, depression, and feelings of worthlessness.

If you believe that you (or others) possess value because you (or they) have beauty, you can so choose. But then you will see yourself as worthless if you have dark hair and you think only blondes have beauty.

Suppose now, you want to add certain facial features to your definition of beauty, which you see as the basis of human worth. Then you can make nose size and shape important. Well, shall you choose as "beautiful" a flat nose, a roundish nose, or a hawkbill nose? How about ear size and shape? Stature and weight distribution? Taste in clothing? You can certainly measure these observable phenomena. The farther you travel upon the pathway of defining worth on the basis of beauty, the more complicated you could make the process and the fewer the number of individuals you begin to see as "beautiful" and "worthwhile." Indeed, you could swiftly eliminate most and perhaps all of the human race.

To complicate the definition further, instead of making worth contingent upon the external beauty, you can add the dimension of academic tool skills, such as reading, writing, and arithmetic. You can set your standards high, and say that we and others rate as "valuable" or "good" when we measure up to your criterion of beauty, and additionally have top-level academic skills.

Going further, you could easily include morality in your ever-expanding definition of "goodness," making the going even tougher than before. Now you look for a person with beauty and academic skill who *also* values truth, fairness, sharing of ideas, compassion, and justice.

But shall you stop there? How about adding some other traits? How about including excellent potential for spatial relations, ability to discover new laws in physics, and a score of .762 on an introversion-extroversion scale of the highest validity? How about resourcefulness, adventurism, and desire for change? How about sexual responsiveness, personal hygiene, love for mother and country? What about neatness, lack of procrastination, and love of life?

What about the past? Perhaps to round out your criteria for the worthwhile person we need data from the past. Maybe a computer could help you with that one! Why not borrow a billion dollars from the sheiks of Arabia and put 100,000 hungry students to work for ten years to develop your program? Don't forget to do a census of the world population, investigate every single person you locate, do a profile card on each, and run every card through the computer to find people of worth. After all, you might find a Cinderella in the foothills of Borneo!

To determine what constitutes a worthy human involves a monumental task—and probably one with no ultimate agreement, because people have widely differing preferences, values, philosophies, and experiences which make any final conclusion most unlikely. Their definitions remain too variable.

What about your finding a person with poor traits worthless? You run into a real problem because you will also tend to look for a *total*ly worthwhile individual. No one seems totally worthwhile, no one appears totally worthless. True, you may find some persons whom, because of certain of their personal qualities, you would prefer to befriend and others, because of their qualities, you would choose to avoid. This shows *your* personal preferences and standards regarding their traits, but does not define them globally as good or bad *people*.

A person who procrastinates about something acts inefficiently in that area. If you feel inconvenienced by his actions, you don't like *that* about him or her and suffer annoyance or frustration. Anything else you say about that person because of his or her procrastinating adds surplus meaning.

Returning once again to the original question: What constitutes human worth? Definition—pure definition. And overgeneralization! If you define your worth on the basis of your procrastination, you will feel anxious, depressed, or inferior whenever you delay a task for a period of time that you deem unreasonable. Thus, you will have congruity between your thoughts, feelings, and actions: You will think yourself no good because you delay, feel anxious over the perceived delay, and delay all the more because of your hassling yourself over your inefficiency. Your belief system obviously will create emotional misery. Furthermore, it does not represent a particularly enlightened or humanistic view but a rigid overgeneralization. Sure, you have the right to make yourself miserable by using this definition, but you can also refuse to rate your total personage on the basis of a very limited criterion.

Rating your behaviors and actions doesn't amount to rating your personal worth. In fact by not rating yourself you can more freely get rid of unvaluable behaviors such as procrastination. For you then focus upon the task, and your "worth" doesn't rise and fall like the stock market at the hint of good or bad news. Instead, you move toward greater joy and efficiency in living.

Acting against procrastination involves giving up berating yourself over flaws and inefficiencies, and focusing on rating only your behaviors and trying to do more of what pleases you and less of what doesn't.

The Yo-Yo Effect

Viewed logically, we cannot determine human value or intrinsic worth on the basis of performance, yet many persons do just that. They fail to recognize that they thereby resort to tautology or arbitrary definition. They also put their "value" on a toboggan slide when they do poorly (e.g., fail to win at chess when they think they should), and they tend to feel grandiose when they meet or exceed their expectations (e.g., win a chess tournament). They over-react and distort reality in both cases by resorting to arrant overgeneralizations.

If you believe your worth mirrors your performance, your feelings go up and down like a Yo-Yo. You put yourself up when your performance matches your standards and down when you fail.

Disputing Self-Devaluating Thoughts

A philosophy of unconditional self-acceptance helps rid you of anxiety, self-anger, or depression. It enables you to take the kinds of risks which let you learn more about your capabilities, to follow your curiosities, to seek mastery over your environment, to develop valuable skills, to enjoy a wider range of emotions.

Employing the ABC method of RET can help deplete your self-derogation tendencies. Whenever you feel worthless because of your inhibition about approaching desirable others, you can dispute your "worthlessness." Rudy can dispute his feelings of inadequacy by asking himself, "What makes me an *inadequate person,* if I fail to approach an attractive woman?" And he can answer, "I never become an *inadequate person,* but only *a person who sometimes acts inadequately.* No evidence exists that I'll always fail. Even if I always failed in the past, I don't *have* to do so in the future. Anyway, if I invariably did fail, how would that make me a bad person? It might indicate that I have an interpersonal handicap and I would find that regrettable. But does that handicap make me a worthless person? It does not!" Only Rudy has the ultimate power to make himself feel inferior. And if he accepts himself with his handicap, he may better identify and try to change that handicap.

Disputing irrational thinking, if you vigorously apply it and don't just thoughtlessly parrot it, can help diminish feelings of inferiority generated from your irrational thoughts. You will then feel more emotionally free and less prone to procrastinate. When you do not deem your worth at stake every time you attempt to do something risky, you have less to lose and more to gain by trying. Even if you continue to procrastinate, you still can learn to accept yourself with your tarrying. Certainly, it will bring disadvantages—but not worthlessness.

By disputing irrational thinking leading to inferiority reactions and procrastination, you can sensibly get off your self-created emotional Yo-Yo. Particularly if you give up angelhood as well. For by doing well you do not rise to heaven. You can legitimately view a fine performance as highly satisfying and pleasant, and a poor one as unpleasant and/or frustrating. But not as angelic or devilish! In order to give up worthlessness, you'd better wisely give up angelhood too!

Summary

You often feel inferior and act procrastinatingly by seeing yourself as rotten. Low self-respect hinders you from broadening your range of experiences and attaining much pleasure.

You derive "self-esteem" from wrongly believing you have a global "essence," and by foolishly rating or labeling this as good or bad, usually on the basis of a few of your successful or unsuccessful performances. This kind of polaristic thinking (evaluating yourself in terms of one end of the goodness-badness scale) almost always interferes with your performances.

A rational solution? Try to surrender the concept of self-rating or self-esteem for a more objective appraisal which includes unconditional self-acceptance. Make yourself "egoless" by evaluating your performances but clearly discriminating between them and your total "essence" or "self." Don't passively accept behaviors and traits that you deem undesirable. Wisely and vigorously work to improve your positive (joy-getting) and diminish your negative (joy-sabotaging) qualities.

By all means, have values. But recognize values as variable, not absolute. Then you can best discriminate between your and others' views of what constitutes the good life and which behaviors will most likely benefit yourself and society.

Instead of seeing the world through a single pair of eyes, make allowances for many different perceptions. You can then give up ego games, particularly the one in which you see yourself as the best judge of what everyone "should" do! You can thereby forego self-rating, overcome procrastination, and attain more of what you want for yourself.

5. Overcoming Procrastination Resulting from Low Frustration Tolerance

Suppose you buy a ticket for the Irish Sweepstakes or a state lottery and fail to win the grand prize by a single numeral. Which emotion will you feel—disappointment, frustration, sadness, anger, or depression?

That depends on your philosophy of life and how you apply it. Any way you look at it, you do experience frustration. You want a million-dollar prize—and you get nothing. Any time you get less than you want, frustration results. If you had no desires, you never would get balked or blocked. If you had constant or overweening desires, you would continually experience thwarting. By wanting or wishing for anything, you automatically make frustration a function of the frequency and the degree of unfulfillment that occurs when you do not get what you desire.

Consequently, if you have a sane philosophy of life—meaning, "I intend to get most of the things I want and to make real efforts to get these things but I realize I can't always get them. So, I'll gracefully accept for the moment what I don't like and work like hell to get what I want in the future"—you may feel only disappointed and frustrated and sad when you encounter significant frustrations.

When, on the other hand, you feel angry or depressed after you have experienced thwarting, you virtually always bring about those inappropriate feelings from a nutty philosophy of life: "I *need* what I want, and other people *should* feel interested enough in me and conditions *should* arrange themselves so I can immediately and completely fulfill my desires. If not, I'll rant and rave until things change. If they never do, I *can't stand* it and might as well die!"

Anger and depression, then, commonly follow frustration. But not necessarily! They do not stem from deprivation itself but from your attitudes, your belief system, *about* it.

Which makes many psychologists, such as John Dollard and Neal Miller, at least partly wrong. Aggression or anger, says the Dollard-Miller hypothesis, follows from frustration. True—it often does. But frustration does not really *lead to* or *cause* aggression, it merely encourages it.

Feelings of frustration may result in enormous benefit. You feel frustrated when you don't know the meaning of a word—so you look it up in the dictionary. Physicians, frustrated by ineffective cures for cancer, persistently keep striving to conquer it. Students, blocked in understanding some classroom concepts, spend more time at their textbooks until they increase their comprehension.

The problem, as we noted in Chapter 2, lies not in your feeling frustrated when you don't learn your arduous homework assignment well, or when one activity (such as study) prevents you from engaging as much as you would like in another activity (such as socializing). It resides in your childishly and grandiosely refusing to tolerate frustration. And low frustration tolerance mainly consists of cognition, an attitude, as well as an unpleasant or uncomfortable feeling.

Your frustration itself, as many psychological theories insufficiently acknowledge, largely stems from your evaluating something as "desirable" or "good." You *decide*, for example, that you "like" or "want" to go swimming with your roommate. Your tastes or preferences partly have biological roots (you have the kind of body that *feels* good when immersed in water instead of one that dislikes immersion) and partly sociological (you learned earlier in life that people tend to enjoy swimming and that they especially enjoy it when accompanied by a pleasant companion; and you learned how to relate to other people, such as your roommate, and to feel happy in their presence).

Still, considering the other potential pleasures (and pains) that you could experience on this particular day, you *decide* or *choose* to go swimming. You *evaluate* this activity as "excellent," "enjoyable," or "healthful." And, comparing it to other things you might do in the same period of time, you *convince* yourself that you will find it preferable. Your *voting* in favor of swimming, and the strength with which you do this voting, have important cognitive elements.

Your degree of frustration involves similar elements. For the more strongly you want to swim, the more intensely frustrated you will feel if you can't. And, when as a result of wanting and getting thwarted you feel deprived, you also tend (although you may not have full awareness of this) to *decide* to focus upon and possibly to enhance your deprivation.

Thus, you have the choice of convincing yourself, (1) "I really did want to go swimming, but now that I find it impractical to do so, I can forget about it and concentrate on other kinds of enjoyments," or (2) "How infuriating! I wanted to go swimming more than anything else in the world today. Just my luck! Maybe it won't kill me to do something else, but nothing will approach the joy I would have had swimming. Damn, damn, damn!"

The second of these convictions, even though it may not include *awfulizing* or unrealistic *demanding,* will tend to make you feel much *more* frustrated than the first one. And the more you dwell on it, the higher your feelings of frustration will tend to rise. If, moreover, you go on to a third, horribilizing set of convictions, you will escalate your frustration still further. You may, in this wise, foolishly conclude: "How *terrible* that I can't go swimming! I really *needed* it. The world shouldn't treat me so unfairly! How can I possibly stand such a deprived, frustrating life?" Just try *these* absolutistic thoughts on for size, and see how enormously your feelings of frustration ascend.

Frustration itself, then, varies in proportion to your *view* of your wants and displeasures, as well as in proportion to your philosophically originated degree of frustration tolerance. You basically choose your own desires—for even if you get "conditioned" early in life to have them, you keep *reconditioning* yourself to continue them. And you decide how much you "want" or "need" to have them fulfilled.

Moreover, you hardly can fail to choose some distinct wants or preferences—since your life would barely seem worth living if you experienced complete desirelessness—and you hardly can fail to experience many impediments to having these preferences consummated. For you just cannot control the many contingencies and events that occur virtually every day. You can have your desires thwarted, for example, by a sudden thunderstorm, by seeing one of your best stocks plummet fifteen points in a few hours, or by having one of your closest associates promise you cooperation and give you nothing. You just can't anticipate or avoid all blocks to your chosen goals. You can't always hold off storms, force stocks to retain their value, or make your friends keep their promises.

To a considerable extent, therefore, you'd better spell *life* as h-a-s-s-l-e. That tends to remain the human condition. If you *accept* this fact—and accept means *accept* and not *like*—you can then do what Herbert Birch found that even chimpanzees can do: use a moderate degree of frustration as a positive emotional impetus to help you do problem solving. Under conditions of low frustration, the chimps seemed to have little incentive to solve problems. Under conditions of high frustration, they also gave up and refused to do much about their problems. But a moderate degree of frustration tended to drive them to work things out better for themselves.

As a higher primate than an ape, you can *choose* to move yourself toward problem solving even under conditions of high frustration. Not that you *have* to. You can decide that the game doesn't seem worth the candle and that you had better withdraw from highly frustrating circumstances. But if the goal seems worthy enough—if you really want to get through graduate school or medical school, for example—you can accept some of the highest levels of frustration and still keep working tenaciously toward it.

Short-Range Hedonism: The Demand for Immediate Gratification

An enormous amount of procrastination ties in with short-range hedonism—the demand that your wants receive immediate gratification and that your feelings of discomfort quickly go away.

Take Susan, for example. She feels exceptionally shy about approaching strangers at a party or in any other kind of social situation. She knows she does not have to live forever with her fearful approach to life; and she keeps promising herself that this time, for once, she will make herself approach others and thereby fight her shyness and develop some better social skills. But every time she thinks of doing so, she pulls back, looks around for someone she already knows, and goes over to talk to that person.

What does Susan tell herself, just prior to backing out on each decision to approach strangers? Mainly: "I know I'll find it hard to go over, and I know it won't remain so hard once I do it enough times. But why must it prove *so* hard to get going? If only I didn't find it *that* hard! Maybe if I hold back and do it more gradually, it will get easier." So, once again, she cops out—and thereby reaffirms her belief about the *too*-hardness of approaching strangers and perpetuates her overwhelming feelings of shyness.

Susan excuses her inertia by telling herself, "People will

probably reject me if I try, so why try?". She spends considerable effort blaming the unfair world for making it so difficult for her to meet other people. How unfair that her parents trained her to feel shy! she thinks, and she finds this unfairness *awful*. She believes she can't tolerate the discomfort of her shyness and reasons that if her parents had given her proper early socializing experience, she would act like "social dynamite" and comfortably meet and speak with whomever she chooses. So she abdicates responsibility for her shyness and procrastination.

If you insist on feeling comfortable in developing social skills, you tend to act against your own best interests. For you normally do not just experience social comfort by the sheer passage of time, but by exposing yourself to "uncomfortable" situations, and by practicing *withstanding* frustration and uneasiness. No law in the universe says you have to feel comfortable *before* approaching a group of people to make their acquaintance. Indeed, you can sensibly dispute this assumed law with: "What makes it so *intolerable* to experience discomfort in approaching a new group?" Answer: "*I* make it 'intolerable' by *defining* it as 'awful' and by *thinking* it 'unbearable.' "

Giving in to almost all your urges signifies low frustration tolerance. You may typically goof on dieting by telling yourself, "It doesn't matter if I temporarily stop dieting. After all, that piece of pizza and a vanilla ice cream cone make too scrumptious a combination to pass up!" You give in to your immediate desire, because you believe, when you feel hungry, that deprivation will make you *too* uncomfortable. Regardless of the elegance of your excuse, you still cop out on dieting. And your subsequent self-damning does not improve your behavior, since when you put yourself down for giving in to the temptation, you often eat all the more to avoid the discomfort you create by inveighing against yourself.

Long-Range Hedonism

As a hedonist, you seek to obtain pleasure and avoid pain. Good! Then you logically recognize that at times you'd better wisely put up with short-term frustrations, in order to assure greater long-term comfort and advantage. But if you devoutly believe you can't tolerate frustration, you may primarily go for short-term comfort, and increase your chances for heightened future discomfort.

Short-range hedonism consists of living for the moment, without due consideration for the future. The student who goes out on a date the night before a major examination, and increases the likelihood of failing, may reason that he couldn't possibly study and deprive himself of the opportunity of going out and having fun. A woman who doesn't want to prepare herself for a career, because the training might take several years, can make herself vocationally unhappy for years doing work she doesn't like. The Ph.D. candidate who sees preliminary examinations as unfair and avoids taking them short-circuits his or her chances for the degree. The business man who doesn't want to take the time to send out mailings to his customers about an upcoming sale will likely suffer fewer sales and less earnings. All these individuals may avoid short-term discomfort, but they actively invite long-range disadvantages by so doing.

Long-range hedonism recognizes that some inconveniences in the present increase chances for a happier and more productive life in the future. If you desire pizza and ice cream, as a long-range hedonist you allow yourself to experience the discomfort of not having what you would like to eat today in order to have the physique you would like tomorrow. A sanely hedonistic student forces himself to study the night before the examination, even though he might have a more pleasurable time on the date. A wise woman prepares herself for a career in spite of the years of training. A person interested in obtaining a Ph.D. degree gracefully accepts the "unfair" preliminary exams that seem irrelevant to future goals. A business man takes the effort to handle his mailings.

You can, of course, *foolishly* continually sacrifice the present for the future. However, you also can sensibly recognize that priorities such as losing weight have more importance than eating pizza. Long-range hedonism does not exclude going to parties, entertaining friends, watching a favorite television show, going on a vacation, or reading interesting novels. It merely means that at times you choose to deprive yourself of some immediate pleasures by viewing them as minor, in comparison to attaining more desirable long-term goals.

The Origins of Low Frustration Tolerance

When infants experience discomfort, they signal their distress by crying. They have minimal tolerance for discomfort and nature has provided them with healthy lungs to help them make known their frustrations. Infants innately seem to try to maintain their existence in a state of comfort.

As you age, you grow more conscious of your world. As you seek stimulation and mastery of your environment, you build up greater frustration tolerance while facing inevitable barriers and blocks. You can't have all the ice cream you'd like. You can't always go to bed when you desire. Teachers give you homework assignments, parents have you wash dishes and tidy up your room. Society pressures you to go out and earn a livelihood. Later, your children make demands upon you. And so life goes. Even death, the end of living, brings unavoidable frustration.

We develop language to express feelings and experiences, and use this same language to predict future events. Thus, not only do you have daily unavoidable frustrations, but you also can *anticipate* frustrations or discomforts when you contemplate doing many things. Depending upon how you view the impediments, you can choose to tolerate the discomfort of engaging in an unpleasant activity or to anguish over anticipated discomfort by believing that you can't *stand* deprivation. Seeing some activity as *too* tough, boring, or frustrating, you may cop out even though if you attempted the task, you *could* stand the experience. The directive nature of language, especially of what you tell yourself (your inner speech), determines whether you divert anticipated frustration into joy-seeking action, or concentrate on evading it.

Frustration tolerance probably includes a biologically or genetically based element related to temperament and stress tolerance. Humans have widely differing temperaments. Some react well to stress, and some badly—and therefore work at amplifying or minimizing discomfort-reduction. Not that low frustration tolerance has no learned element. It certainly has! But it also seems to have a large constitutional component.

This means . . . what? Simply that people with strong innate tendencies toward procrastination had better work harder to overcome the problem than those who have less trouble meeting deadlines. Unfair! you say. Whether fair or unfair, the cookie still crumbles that way! And no easy or magical solution exists. You almost always can overcome your "lazy" tendencies. But the process of change involves considerable *work* in developing more of a long-range hedonistic outlook. Yes, w-o-r-k!

The Instant-Solution Myths

You may find it simple to avoid discomfort for the time being and to obtain many of the good things in life with a rapidity and ease that would have astonished granny. The credit-card revolution has made it possible for you, as long as you work, to acquire what your heart desires as quickly as you can sign your name. No longer need you save for a new living-room set. Just open a revolving charge, use BankAmericard, or take out an easy loan. Simple? Sure! But add the new payment on top of your auto installments, your mortgage, and your myriad other monthly charges, and short-term ease often aggravates your long-term debt at interest rates that have helped make the American credit industry the wealthiest in the world.

The credit market "capitalizes" on a philosophy of short-range hedonism. But it doesn't stand alone. Madison Avenue also capitalizes on the quest for instant solutions. One TV commercial has a miracle pill turning a person acting tyrannically and bitchily into a loving angel. Another commercial reveals how a quick spritz of deodorant spray will whisk all a woman's troubles away. Another ad shows how a tiny blue pill can promote a night of blissful comfort and restful, peaceful slumber. And don't forget!—nothing surpasses sucking in a lungful of Snarlborough smoke and nicotine in the pollution-free air of the country with one's loving mate cancerously puffing away (on a Schmucky Strike, of course) as you both revel beside a majestic waterfall. Remember the hand lotion ad that implied that seven days of use would lead to lovlier hands, followed by a wedding scene with the happy user about to depart on her honeymoon with her handsome new husband? More of the media hogwash that fosters a belief in magic and encourages low frustration tolerance!

The food-processing industry has long promoted quickly prepared goodies that not only drain homemakers' pocketbooks but pollute their systems with preservatives and other non-nutritional fillers. Do such ads *create* many people's belief that they utterly need ease and comfort? No, but they take full advantage of our innate and acquired tendencies to think gullibly and to seek enormous ease. They thereby help augment our short-range hedonistic view and our "need" for avoiding frustration, even though we bring on greater discomfort and anguish later.

Whining and Complaining

When you foster low tolerance for frustration, you distress yourself over minor impediments and tend to whine and complain about the inequities of life. Sobbing statements take over, such as: "How unfair and awful!" "I shouldn't have to do this!" "Why does everybody have it easy but me?" "I don't want to do it because I find it boring, and I *can't stand* boredom!" These reflect an attitude of low frustration tolerance, which often leads to procrastination—and then to more complaining!

When you chronically complain, you may not only alienate yourself from others but the friends you keep will likely manifest a similar attitude and encourage your and their neurosis. Your reciprocal sobbing about the unfairness of life leads to loss of much pleasure.

To rid yourself of chronic frustration-enhancing thoughts like, "I can't stand this!" ask yourself, "*Why* can't I stand what I don't like?" A well-thought-through answer results in: "Sure, I *can* stand washing my automobile or studying for a test! I may never like them, but I *can* bear them!"

Similarly, you may ask, "What about the world indicates that it must treat me fairly?" Answer: "It has *no* reason for treating me other than as it does!"

You do not design questions like these to make you feel good about an unpleasant situation—but to undermine the irrational thinking that makes you foolishly procrastinate. And since, after giving up your *demands* for pleasure and fairness, you still *want* such things, you can wisely force or push yourself into activity that helps you avoid future discomfort and gain greater advantage. Where your whining promotes procrastination, your pushing stops it. So use your energy *doing* instead of *stewing*.

Case Examples of Low Frustration Tolerance and Procrastination

Sylvia behaved like an infant who insists on instant comfort, suffers delayed gratification, and escalates her frustration by bawling that she can't stand an inconvenience. Because such a child demands an instant solution for discomfort, she intolerantly wails when no easy answer turns up.

A bright and unusually attractive young woman, Sylvia

would often attend as many as ten parties a week looking for a handsome, cultured, well-mannered, life-loving man. She pictured their falling in love with each other immediately and achieving instant intimacy.

She had exciting relationships for a short time, but passion rapidly faded when a given male failed to move into a marital future with dispatch. When a relationship dissolved, she would whine and sob about her plight, then go out and try again, only to repeat the same unhappy pattern. While Sylvia did not procrastinate about meeting men, she reacted intolerantly to the frustrations of having her intimate relationships move slowly. She procrastinated about working at developing greater frustration tolerance, and she avoided looking at the impact her behavior had on those with whom she desired intimacy. The less she got what she wanted the more babyishly she behaved, demanding that she have what she wanted when she wanted it. She felt sure she *couldn't stand* feeling thwarted. So she stood it forever!

Consider Dan's case. Rather than pursue his goal of a core relationship, Dan copped out entirely from finding a woman with whom he could establish that relationship. He rarely made any systematic attempt to meet people. His excuse: He found the process too tough and it took too long. Like Sylvia, he wanted "things to start happening." Unlike Sylvia, he even felt unwilling to initiate the effort to go after his goal. This same pattern evidenced itself in his avoiding training for an electronics job after high school graduation, because the program took two years to complete and that seemed "too long." He despised his job as mechanic's helper but kept doing it, while complaining that he should have started years before on electronics.

While Dan fears failure, he remains intolerant of discomfort when it comes to meeting people and furthering his career. He nets *more* frustration and dissatisfaction than if he had forced himself to get moving.

Both Sylvia and Dan remain short-sighted, short-range hedonists. To avoid momentary discomfort, they take what appears the easy way out. This failure to take a long-range hedonistic view, and to give up present pleasure for future gain leads to procrastination.

When you avoid dealing with your frustrations, you often retard satisfaction and enjoyment. By labeling discomfort as "too tough," you make it *more* painful. Thus, you avoid immediate pain—but simultaneously miss the positive excitement and sense of satisfaction which can result from mastering difficult situations.

Expressions like "I don't want to do it," "I can't," and "It seems just too hard," lead to infantile avoidance of discomfort. This kind of procrastination represents a primitive mode of responding. And if you let your onerous work pile up, and if you down yourself for this, you tend to aggravate your pain and trouble.

The Pile-Up

Maude, in avoiding doing dishes, throwing out newspapers, meeting new people, and getting over her whiny mode of interacting, often felt overwhelmed with mounds of undone work. Her frustrations and immobility increased as she witnessed the consequences of her delays. It just seemed too hard to get her work done, yet too difficult to tolerate her disarrayed life. Faced with her mountain of tasks, she would stay home one weekend to catch up on her housekeeping. But Monday morning would find her apartment still messy—in spite of her having deprived herself of going out and having fun. Her conflict about feeling intolerant of the condition of her apartment, and of herself for not doing anything about it, created much unnecessary anguish. Typical of many who persistently procrastinate! They increasingly feel overwhelmed, then dawdle for extended periods of time worrying over where to begin, and thus pile up more work.

To break her pattern of inaction, Maude hired a cleaning person for a day to heave out the papers, wash the dishes, and generally straighten out the apartment. She then had a clean apartment that she felt she could keep reasonably tidy. She arranged to have the cleaning person work on a once-a-month basis, and found that she could do the rest of the work herself. While not an elegant solution, it proved much better than self-damning. She could more elegantly have questioned her nonsense about proving worthless and incompetent because of her procrastination. But at least she stopped telling herself that she found it "too hard" to clean her apartment, and she did wisely force herself to help clean it.

Other Aspects of Low Frustration Tolerance

We already have considered some of the major irrational beliefs that will produce low frustration tolerance and tend to encourage procrastination. Some variations on these beliefs, with methods of disputing and surrendering them, follow.

1. Constant "need" for excitement.

IRRATIONAL BELIEFS: "I need constant stimulation. I just can't stand boredom. If any of my tasks seem too monotonous, I can't bear it. So I'll put it off until it seems more exciting."

DISPUTING: "In what way do I need constant stimulation? Why can't I stand boredom and monotonous jobs? When will such tasks seem more exciting?"

EFFECT: "Obviously I don't need constant stimulation, though I'd sure like it. Fat chance! Boredom remains an almost inescapable fact of life, and many important chores have boring aspects. Tough! I *can* bear monotonous tasks—I have done so plenty of times up to now. Too bad they exist but they do! Since I find dull jobs so tiring, I'd better finish them quickly, and not dawdle over them and make them *more* monotonous. Why not get them over with as quickly and efficiently as feasible so I can get on to more exciting things?"

2. Need to feel like doing difficult activity

IRRATIONAL BELIEFS: "They shouldn't give me such tight deadlines on writing up my chemistry experiments when I don't feel like doing it. How unfair! I'll wait until I feel like doing it. Then it will seem easier, and I won't mind it so much. To hell with them! I'll just wait."

DISPUTING: "Why shouldn't they give me work that I don't feel like doing? What law of the universe states that they must only give me work when I want to do it? Who has writ that unfairness must not exist? Granted, it may seem easier to do this work if I wait until I feel like doing it, but will I really benefit myself by waiting?"

EFFECT: "Obviously, they have every right to give me work I don't feel like doing—even if I can prove them wrong in giving it. No law states that they must only give me work when I want it. Unfairness *does* exist—and quite frequently. I could wait to do this work until I really feel like doing it—but who knows when that time will come? And if I wait for that eventuality, I will likely do myself much more harm than good. So had I not better get off my rump and do it *now*?"

3. The need for inspiration.

IRRATIONAL BELIEFS: "If I do this essay now, just to complete it on time, I won't feel inspired to do it. And, to do it well, I really need inspiration. So I'd better put it off until inspiration strikes me, and then I'll do the best damned essay I possibly can."

DISPUTING: "Why do I *need* inspiration to do a good essay? Why *must* I do this one superbly? Will putting off the essay now necessarily mean I'll feel inspired to do it later?"

EFFECT: "I don't need inspiration to do a good essay—though I would find it nice if I happened to have it. Nor do any reasons exist why I have to do this one very well. The course only requires a passably good paper, and I don't have to impress my teacher or my classmates with an outstanding one. Putting off doing the essay right now and waiting for inspiration to occur won't necessarily work anyway—it may never occur. Or it may occur right away, in the course of my forcing myself to write at this moment. So, inspiration or no inspiration, I'd better stop my nonsense and do the blasted essay!"

4. The need for a vacation.

IRRATIONAL BELIEFS: "I have too much work to do and perhaps will have a breakdown if I don't get some time off from it. I definitely need a vacation. How awful to have so many things on my back all at once!"

DISPUTING: "Granted that I have a great deal of work now, what makes it *too* much? Why must I suffer a breakdown if I don't get some time off from it? What evidence exists that I truly need a vacation? What makes it awful to have so many things on my back all at once?"

EFFECT: "Nothing makes it *too* much work—just *much*. Maybe I won't have the time or energy to finish all the work I have, but at worst I simply will do less than I would prefer to do. It won't kill me to fail to finish it all, and I won't have a breakdown if I stick at it. I could certainly use a vacation, but why do I *need* it? I don't! Nothing makes it awful to have so many things on my back all at once. Inconvenient and disadvantageous, yes. But *awful* means *more than* inconvenient—and nothing can amount to 101% inconvenient, obnoxious, or disadvantageous. *Awful* also means that this inconvenient thing must not exist. But if it does, it does. Tough!"

5. The need to have onerous tasks evaporate.

IRRATIONAL BELIEFS: "I can't stand this library reading assignment! If I keep putting it off, maybe my professor will forget about it. Maybe she'll get replaced by another woman who will cancel the assignment. Maybe she'll drop dead of a heart attack."

DISPUTING: "In what way can't I stand reading in the library? What probability exists that my professor will forget the assignment, get replaced by another woman, or drop dead? Perhaps I'll never like reading in the library, but do I have to wail about it and make it *that* hard?"

EFFECT: "Of course I can stand reading it in the library—though I may never find it pleasant. The chances of my professor forgetting the assignment, quitting her job, or dropping dead seem remote, and I'd better assume they won't materialize. I don't have to wail about the hardship of reading in the library and make it even more unpleasant. I'd better hop to it and get done with it!"

Summary

Practically no one likes frustration—wanting *x* and getting less. As you try to survive and feel happy, one of your main goals consists of minimizing frustration and maximizing pleasure. Therefore, feeling deprived or blocked has constructive aspects. It motivates you to undo the blocking and rid yourself of the deprivation. "Necessity," says the old proverb, "proves the mother of invention." Not quite!—for if you think you *need* or *must have* something you lack, you can throw yourself into such a state of rage and panic that you invent nothing but those disruptive emotions—hardly a way out of your thwarted state!

Why not, then, try to change the adage to: "Desire and the attendant frustration can sire invention." This seems especially true when you make your desires follow a long-range as well as a short-range pattern, and sometimes choose to select future goals over short-term pathways. For you can find happiness in both immediate and preplanned pursuits. The main trick: Don't consistently sacrifice the latter for the former. Procrastination doesn't always imply an addiction to short-range hedonism. Only about 98% of the time!

6. Overcoming Procrastination Resulting from Hostility

As noted in Chapter 2, procrastination may result from feelings of hostility, and hostility may also serve as a rationalization for procrastinating, We shall deal in this chapter with some of the links between hostility and needless delay of important projects and show how you can overcome procrastination that ties in with anger, resentment, and passive aggression.

Understanding Hostility-Created Procrastination

You make yourself hostile when you grandiosely demand (instead of normally desire) that others let you have your way and when you intolerantly damn them when they thwart you. When you surrender yourself to this kind of childish grandiosity, you frequently spend inordinate amounts of time in resentful brooding, in plotting and scheming revenge, and in over-rebelliously acting against the people or things you hate.

The time and energies you thus consume get taken away from constructive pursuits. For how, if you seethe against your parents, friends, or teachers, can you healthfully focus on your school work—or on anything else? Not very easily!

Not that anger has no constructive aspects whatever. It may motivate you to fight and work against various kinds of frustrations and injustices, and sometimes plays an important part in righting social wrongs. But it consists of two main components, with only one of them in the realm of reason. That one we call strong displeasure and determination to change obnoxious occurrences.

Suppose you agree with your roommate that you will only use your apartment for socializing purposes before 9:00 P.M. on weekdays, and that after that time you both will remain reasonably quiet and study or at least allow the other to do so in peace. He solidly concurs—and then insists on inviting guests in after 9:00 P.M. on a good number of weekdays.

If you act wisely, you then say to yourself something along these lines: "Cripes! There he goes again, breaking the rule we set up only a few weeks ago. What a pain! I wish he acted more considerately and hate his behaving so thoughtlessly. I feel determined to do something about this and to get him back on our original track. Now let's see what I can do to persuade him to live up to our agreement!"

If you stay with such thoughts as these—and don't go beyond them—you will feel highly displeased with your roommate's behavior and quite determined to get him to change it. You will not, however, feel truly angered or enraged. Such feelings will emanate mainly from some additional, foolish self-verbalizations, such as: "How can he so unfairly break those rules, especially when we only recently established them! He *shouldn't* act that way! What a lousy bastard! I'll fix his wagon!"

With absolutistic, demanding, condemning thoughts like these, you'll easily make yourself angry. And then, enraged, you may deliberately refuse to study, claiming that your roommate prevents you from doing so or that he ruins your mood to do so. Perhaps more importantly, while inwardly or outwardly railing against him, you hardly will feel in the mood to study, will have little time or energy left for doing it, and (ironically!) will turn yourself off from virtually any thought of studying while you presumably try to protect your right to do so.

If you have a procrastination problem to begin with, your anger almost always will help you enhance it. For instead of admitting that you have the problem, you can rationalizingly blame your roommate (and other grim circumstances) for causing it, and can cop out on trying to do very much about it.

The solution? First, get rid of your anger. Ask yourself: "Why *can't* my roommate so inconsiderately and unfairly break the recently established rules that we have agreed to set up?" Answer: "Of course he can! In fact, he seems to have a rare talent at breaking such rules—or interpreting them so that he doesn't think they apply to him. How can he break them? Easily! With no trouble whatever."

Ask yourself: "Where can I find evidence that my roommate *shouldn't* act the way he does? and how can I legitimately call his acts *horrible?*" Answer: "Nowhere can I find such evidence. I may prove him *wrong* for ignoring our agreement. But I might as well have asked Hitler to love the Jews as him to act in accordance with our agreement. In what way *should* a wrongdoer act rightly? In no way at all!"

Second answer: "I cannot legitimately designate his acts as horrible. As obnoxious and unpleasant, yes—definitely disadvantageous to me. As unfair and inconsiderate, yes—for he has broken our agreement. But a *horrible* act means one that proves *more than* obnoxious and inconsiderate; and one that *should not, must not* exist *because* I find it unfair. Well, do I run the universe? Not yet! So I can only legitimately see his act as wrong and obnoxious—but I'd better stop inventing any more-than-wrongness, any *horror* to attach to it."

Ask yourself: "What makes my roommate a lousy bastard?" Answer: "Nothing does. His *acts* may have a bastardly quality but I cannot legitimately rate *him* as a total, global, once-and-for-all-time bastard. Moreover, if I call him a bastard, I don't only mean that he does rotten acts, but that he does so unnaturally, against the laws of the universe; and that therefore he deserves suffering and damnation, which the universe presumably will give him. Claptrap! No law of the universe says he must not act rottenly, that he turns subhuman if he does, or that he gets eternally damned if he acts that way. Only *my* law says that—and my law seems very, very nutty if it does! So I'd better stick to rating his rotten traits and not defame him, in toto, as a *rotten person*."

In other words, if you feel angry or enraged at your roommate, and you directly or indirectly procrastinate in connection with this anger, first work against your anger-creating cognitions, and then try to stop your procrastinating. Once you rid yourself of your anger, you at least give up *that* reason for procrastinating about studying.

Let us consider the case of Judy—who beautifully displayed how anger often goes with procrastination. Judy's anger originated in her natural tendencies to command that the world go her way and to react with rage when it did not, as well as from a stressful home environment which created conditions to which she could easily over-react.

Her mother, a "self-sacrificing" person, let the world know how much she kept struggling and suffering. The father, an alcoholic, chronically whined and complained about the unfairness of the world for keeping a brilliant fellow like himself down. When not complaining about the world, he spent much of his time criticizing Judy. So for years, Judy dreamed of punishing both parents for "ruining my life" and preoccupied herself thinking hateful thoughts about them.

Despite high intelligence, Judy graduated in the lowest quarter of her high school class. She partly did so to get back at her father, who enormously valued achievement. Both parents believed Judy disgraced them by her low grades, while she kept insisting that they must accept her with these grades. She also proved to them that they could not force her to work harder. Frustrated and angered, they forced her to visit several psychiatrists—till she again proved that no one could make her change.

She decided to go to college and sent out numerous applications. Despite her excellent College Board scores, her poor high school record killed her chances of going to the schools of her choice. She blamed her parents for "screwing up my life and causing me to end up in a second-rate school."

Once she was in college, her parents hoped she would get married—and relieve them of all responsibility. But Judy rarely dated, gained forty pounds, and blamed her parents for teaching her poor eating habits. When she did bring a man home to meet her parents, she always chose one they found appalling. She met some men she desired to date and marry who might have proved acceptable to her parents, but her obese appearance and angry manner turned them off.

The rebelliousness Judy exhibited toward her parents, she also exhibited toward herself. She took positions below her capabilities. For instance, having earned a degree in social work, she worked as a secretary. In this position, she would damn herself for her weak secretarial performance and for working as a secretary when she had a Master's degree in social work. She would insist to herself that she must first improve her secretarial skills and then find a job as a social worker. But she rebelled against her own demands by doing neither.

This same pattern of oppositionalism, which resulted in procrastination, showed itself in Judy's eating. When she *demanded* that she diet, she would pigheadedly balk, eat all the more, then command that she stop overeating. Endless repetition of pattern!

Judy lived a very restricted and procrastination-filled life. Her anger and brooding resentment resulted in her depriving herself of many things she wanted. True, she successfully opposed and rebelled against her parents when an adolescent. But now she continued to deprive herself, as she so deeply blamed the world that she rarely paused to examine the impact of her philosophy and behavior upon herself.

Judy kept cutting off her nose to spite her face; and even when she recognized this, she struggled many months before she began to overcome her anger and to work in her own self-interest. She could never make up for her years of procrastination, but she could, with therapy, lead herself to many enjoyable and fulfilling future experiences.

Judy finally, after working at therapy as she had never worked at anything before, changed significantly along several lines: First, she stopped viewing her parents as worthless skunks, realized that they had serious problems of their own, and saw that, with these problems, one might expect them to treat her just as badly as they did. Their treatment constituted a logical deduction from their own irrational premises, from which no other kind of treatment could probably have emerged.

Second, Judy worked at accepting herself rather than constantly striving for the approval of others. She still wanted to do her job well, but not to prove that others could accept her and that she thereby had value as a human. She now mainly wanted to do it for her own satisfaction—to get better results and to enjoy herself more.

Third, she decided that she didn't have to prove herself by controlling others. Even though some of her changes, such as losing weight, would also please her parents, she gave up her attempts to spite them and thereby put them in their place, and felt happy both in her loss of weight and in their delight in it.

Fourth, Judy decided that she could tolerate various inconveniences and frustrations, without ranting about those who helped bring them about. She still disliked doing many things at the menial secretarial job she had, but she worked at *only* disliking them and not at commanding that they cease to exist. Meanwhile, she prepared herself to enter the social work profession and stoically undertook some rather boring but necessary refresher courses.

Fifth, Judy gave up her fantasy of starring as a great actress—something she had done nothing about even though she dreamed about it constantly—and agreed with herself that the world didn't owe her anything, including fame and fortune, and that she'd better stick to her last, social work, and see what she could do for herself.

In more ways than one, then, Judy worked against her self-downing, her low frustration tolerance, and her hostility to others, especially to her parents. From an over-rebellious, sullen, and continually balky individual, she turned into a rather cooperative, self-caring person who could much more logically pursue her goals.

Procrastination and Passive-Aggressiveness

You may at times show your anger in passive-aggressive behavior that takes the form of procrastination. Instead of expressing your resentment at others directly, this kind of behavior enables you to do so indirectly. Thus, when driving on highways you can display a classic form of passive-aggressive procrastination by traveling in the "fast" lane at a snail's pace, thereby forcing other automobiles to pile up behind you. Sometimes you may daydream and unwittingly slow down traffic, but you also may brim over with demands and convince yourself they hold water. After all, you travel at the "right" limit, and to hell with those who want to speed! Occasionally, you have opportunities to play more traffic games, when an impatient motorist tailgates you. You can then slow down even more, or flash your brake lights to get back. Finally, if cut off by an overly aggressive driver, you can tell yourself that the other driver should not drive so dangerously and can try to punish this villain by tailgating, horn-blowing, shouting, or pulling sharply in front of him and cutting him off.

Passive-aggressive procrastinators act badly, not only to others, but to themselves. The professor angry at the administration, and fearful of expressing his anger directly, may take it out on his students with dull, disorganized lectures. Not only does he inconvenience the students, but he blocks his own developing greater skills in his subject, and quietly gnaws away at his gut in the process, by dwelling upon administrative unfairness.

How do you cope with passive-aggressiveness and the procrastination with which you may link it? First, by recognizing that all aggression or hostility doesn't include extreme verbalism or violent action. You can feel inwardly angry without saying or doing anything to your "enemy." Similarly, you can express rage silently and passively, without cursing people or lashing out at them physically.

When someone pries "too much" into your life, you can mildly tell him or her, "I would rather not answer your questions. I like to keep my own counsel." Or you can angrily say, "Look, you son of a bitch! What I do and feel remains none of your goddamn business!"

Passively-aggressively, however, you can also give monosyllabic answers, avoid the questions, query your questioner in a negative manner, joke about busybodies, or do several other hostile, avoidant things in a quiet, subtle way. If so, recognize your behavior as hostile. Acknowledge to yourself that you feel quite negative toward your "persecutor."

Second—in the usual rational-emotive manner—get to the source of your hostility. Assuming that your questioner acts wrongly, has he or she *no right* to act that way? *Must* you immediately get him or her off your back? Does failing to answer this person, or procrastinating about directly dealing with the questioning, *really* solve your problem about it? Will your passive-aggressive attitude and behavior get you as many good and as few bad results as you would like to get? What alternative method of response might work better?

As usual, try to see your passive-aggressive attitude and the procrastination that may accompany it as your own choice—not something forced on you. Not something you have to do. Not something that must work, even if you defeat yourself in the process. No: a plan of action—really of *attack*—that you have probably foolishly decided upon. Something you have chosen to do and can choose to stop doing. In the long run, what will you get out of using it? Figure out the best answer to this kind of question, rather than how to do your "opponent" in at all costs.

Finally, when you merely feel displeased rather than enraged about another's conduct, decide on a plan of words and action. And decide on one that avoids defensive excuses like procrastination!

Anger and the Ability to Control Situations

Do you think the solution to your problems resides in changing environmental contingencies to coincide with your personal wishes, and that you have the power to do this? If so, then you see the locus of control as internal. On the other hand, if you think the fates control your destiny, you may tend to believe in astrology and predestination, and to see yourself as helpless in turning the tide of your personal history.

Neither of these extreme viewpoints holds true in all conditions, as locus of control proves multidimensional. Some conditions make external factors more potent, as when the accident of birth launches you in a social class with minimal opportunities for getting training in a profession. But even in such circumstances, given ability and motivation, you can exert some control over your destiny by working very hard to lift yourself out of your social stratum.

If you procrastinate and see yourself as externally controlled, you tend to blame outside forces for your troubles and feel not only angry but helpless and vulnerable: "I can't do anything about what happens." If you procrastinate and view yourself as an internal controller, you tend to act intropunitively by blaming yourself and feeling guilt and self-anger.

Seeing yourself as externally controlled, you have many built-in excuses for procrastination: "If only my folks hadn't brought me into the world . . . if I had a better upbringing . . . if people had taught me Spanish!" In short, you see factors outside of your immediate control as totally responsible and yourself as blameless but hopeless. Seeing yourself as an internal controller, you may take on all blame for your deficiencies or poor life conditions and totally condemn yourself. Or you can combine both these extreme views and feel convinced that (1) you *should* control your destiny and you rate as weak and despicable when you don't and (2) things remain out of hand and you cannot possibly control your life, so you might as well give in to apathy and inertia. Any of these foolish beliefs may lead you to "curse the darkness rather than light one candle."

When you assume that you don't control your destiny, but that outside forces (including people who seem connected with these forces) control you, you may take the path of angering yourself against these forces. Instead of directly making yourself apathetic and inert—"Why bother to get moving and change my lot, when these greater forces will wind up controlling me anyway?"—you tend to fume against external controls that you define as implacable and unchangeable.

Your irrational beliefs then run along these lines: "I can do nothing about my professor's compulsively making me and the rest of the class do an inordinate amount of work for his crummy course. He enjoys making us suffer and will go on acting sadistically no matter what I do. Okay, I'll show him! If I can't do anything about getting him to change, at least I can sabotage his goals. I'll refuse to do what he wants—and refuse to suffer the way he wants us to suffer. I'll just get by with a minimum of work, and show him that he can't really control me and that I will get along happily in spite of his sadism. Blast him!"

With this kind of hostile rebelliousness, you fool yourself by giving up control, on the one hand, but partly taking it back (actually, *falsely* taking it back) through supposedly winning an ego battle with your controller. Since you attribute hostile motives that this person may not have, and since you also invent an ego victory that your "persecutor" may not even notice, you really "conquer" your own fantasied "villains." In the process, you procrastinate or fail to complete a task that, if gotten out of the way, would provide you with a good deal of control over yourself, if not over others.

The solution? Stop attributing motives to other that they may not have and bring yourself back to the real problem, when conditions remain somewhat out of your control, of managing things as best you can. As Rimm and Masters show, you can check your own attributions and question whether or not they seem valid. In the case just hypothesized, you could ask yourself: "Does my professor really have sadistic motives? Granted the work he gives us may seem too much, but does he give it because he wants us to suffer? Or does he give it for some other reason which has little or nothing to do with the students? Perhaps he has his own perfectionistic tendencies. Perhaps he honestly believes that much work will do us good. Perhaps he doesn't realize how little time we have. What other motives than sadism might he have?"

Going further than this, you can attack your hostility and over-rebelliousness by using the common RET technique of supposing the worst, and showing yourself that you *still* do not have to upset yourself about it. You can do this kind of thinking:

"Suppose my professor really has sadistic tendencies and wants to control us and make us squirm. Suppose we can do nothing about this, and cannot get the administration to induce him to change. Why must I still anger and defeat myself by trying to show him that he can't get away with this?"

"I don't have to win this kind of Pyrrhic victory and show him anything. He has his problems, if I hypothesize correctly. Okay—so he has his problems! He has a perfect right, as a fallible human person, to act wrongly. Just as I have a right to act equally wrongly—and do myself in by raging against him. Too bad that he acts the way he does—but he *does!* Now, if I can accept him with his obnoxious sadistic traits, I can probably best get myself out of this dilemma. I may succeed in buttering him up and getting some kind of special dispensation about doing so much work. Or I can do it minimally but adequately, and still pass the course. Or I can do the work thoroughly and well—and perhaps benefit myself by doing it that way, even if he receives sadistic satisfaction from seeing me work so hard.

"Several possibilities exist for my solving this problem—*if* I stop upsetting myself about the fact that he has created it. Fascinating, how the world can have so much unfairness! Now, how can I behave fairly to *myself*, in the face of this kind of unfairness, and thereby get along much better in life?"

By seeing the thing in this worst possible light, and nonetheless determining not to upset yourself about it, you will at least find it possible to remove *your* problem of over-reacting from *the world's* problem of remaining unfair, and your resentment and over-rebelliousness will tend to vanish. This fundamental attitude, that you *will* cope with the unpleasantries of the universe and that you *will* evolve a workable solution that, even if not good or great, reduces rather than increases these unpleasantries, brings about a rational approach to anger that will serve you well. Don't think that, utopianly, you will never make yourself enraged about any of the injustices of life. Sometimes you will! But, compared to what you usually "unthinkingly" do in this respect—for, actually, you unconsciously if not consciously *think* your way into every resentful position you hold—you will improve considerably. Try it. See!

Summary

Anger, hostility, and resentment ally themselves with procrastination either by directly or indirectly causing it or tend to get used as excuses or rationalization for self-sabotaging delay. In arriving at the real source of such anger and in attempting to change it, you'd better first fully admit that you create and invent it. Not that conditions may not contribute to your angering yourself against people or things; they may. But the pin you stick in your hand doesn't *make you* hurt. *You* hurt yourself by weilding the pin, just as *you* assuage the pain by pulling it out of your hand. Lots of things, events, and people contribute to your hostile feelings, but you cop out on admitting your *own* responsibility for these feelings when you devoutly believe that *they* anger you.

In connection with procrastination linked with anger, admit your own culpability. See exactly what you tell yourself to create your rage. Find the *shoulds, oughts, musts, demands* that you foist on others and on the world. And fight them! Dispute them, challenge them, uproot them! Watch your attribution of nasty motives to others. But even if they do clearly treat you unfairly, and even if they consciously mean to do so, *your* taking them overly seriously and *your* commanding that they not do what they indubitably have done— these remain the real issues. Deal with yourself before you try to correct the unfairnesses of others. Then, unhostilely, you will have a much better chance to get some of the results you want.

7. Overcoming Other Emotional Problems Resulting in Procrastination

We thus far have outlined three main emotional difficulties leading to and stemming from procrastination; and practically all other disturbances that we can think of can go under these three major headings. Quite commonly, however, other disturbed feelings—such as perfectionism, the dire need for love, anxiety, guilt, shame, and depression—also have a significant role in the causation of needless delay. These disturbances mainly fall under the heading of self-downing. But since they seem important in their own right, we shall consider in this chapter how you can specifically handle them if and when they arise.

Perfectionism

As rational-emotive therapy writings have emphasized from the very beginning, perfectionistic philosophies lie at the very root of disordered emotions. Paul Dubois noted this many years ago, and so did Alfred Adler and Karen Horney. In fact, Horney, who had a way with words, invented the terms *idealized image* (to show that humans tend to romanticize their view of themselves) and *the tyranny of the shoulds* (to indicate that they largely demand that they *have to*, instead of state they would very much *like to*, do well and win others' approval).

When you demand perfection of yourself and others, you tend to give yourself a hard time if you or they fail to live up to the unrealistic standards you set. No matter how hard you or they try, both of you "fail"—because you think that you or they *should have* done better.

As a fallible human person, you will make many mistakes and have many less-than-godlike performances. Your rigid insistence on meeting objectives "perfectly" will often encourage self-condemnation and withdrawal. Worse!—by linking your worth to the star of outstanding achievement, you may give yourself considerable anxiety and depression.

You may reveal perfectionism without suffering from compulsive meticulousness. Instead, a perfectionist philosophy may show itself in overly casual performances—as when you refuse to risk imperfect acts—and therefore "casually" avoid failure by just going through the motions of life. You may, like some problem children, look at a book for long periods of time without ever reading any of the lines, hurriedly put down just any answer on tests, or cut up during instruction periods that you believe you won't master. You may act like the man with the sloppy office desk who "nonchalantly" puts himself down because he doesn't keep his work area tidy. Or like the student who pretends she'll feel satisfied with a C grade because she finds the course "trivial." The common perfectionistic factor you hold with these people consists of the attitude or belief that you rate as stupid or no good if your performances reach less than desired heights.

*Must*urbation constitutes the mental virus inherent in perfectionism. You demand that you *must* perform adequately—and thus throw yourself into an anxiety state or other kind of emotional tailspin. You can even turn a simple situation in which you would like to express your feelings or point of view into one of intense *must*urbating.

As a perfectionist you have one main—and sacred—philosophy: "I *have to* rate as a good person! And to achieve this, I *must* perform well or outstandingly." Also, "Others, to have goodness as people, *must* perform perfectly." Usually, the perfectionistic individual has real bigotry.

This philosophy leads to a sense of uncertainty where you avoid change of any sort unless you have some iron-clad assurance that the new behavior will bring you exactly what you want, and with minimum distress. Naturally, since you have no such guarantees, you dillydally forever. And display low frustration tolerance!

Perfectionism, of course, has antidotes. Basically, you'd better convince yourself that (1) perfect performances may have their advantages, but you can rarely or never attain them; (2) however desirable, you don't *have to* accomplish them; (3) even when some of your acts seem perfect, *you* remain an imperfect, predictably fallible person; (4) your worth as an individual does not relate to the perfection of your deeds. If you can get yourself to believe these philosophies and keep eliminating the crazy belief that you only can accept yourself and consider yourself worthy of life and happiness when you act perfectly, you will save yourself a good deal of self-denigration. With it minimized or gone, you take away most of the reasons for procrastinating about something that you might easily do (and in all probability will do) in a decidedly imperfect way.

The Dire Need for Love

A considerable amount of your procrastinating may stem from your love lushness—your dire need for others' approval and your extreme avoidance of anything you think they won't love you for doing. For, you may foolishly ask yourself, how could people you find significant *really* accept you if you behave unideally? And feeling strongly that they couldn't, you may refrain from doing almost anything risky in their presence. This, of course, won't tend to work very well: The people whose love you think you "need" will then probably disapprove of you for avoiding or postponing various things that they would like you to do or that they consider normal. But, torn between obtaining their disapproval for doing something poorly and not doing it at all, you frequently will view the former brand of censure as much worse than the latter brand, and will procrastinate and procrastinate.

As a love lush, you may get high on the approval of others, just as the alcoholic gets high on booze; and you may feel anxious or depressed (psychologically hung over) if you don't get the reactions you think you need. You can even assume that, because you don't act well or perfectly, others *must* dislike you; and you can immensely upset yourself with this silly fiction.

You can help your love lushing lead to procrastination— and, incidentally to reproduce and sustain itself—by assuming that if you do things promptly, others will hate you for doing the wrong thing, for doing the right thing badly— or even for acting nonprocrastinatingly. Of course, they may. But your problem, the one that really makes you procrastinate in these instances, derives from magical belief that you must find it *awful* and will turn into a rotten person if these others criticize or despise you. Keep *that* thought, and make a few of the above assumptions, and you will dawdle like hell!

Joe's behavior illustrates this problem. When some employees struck his corporation for higher wages, Joe felt worried because he thought he would let his supervisor down if he walked out with his co-workers. But he also feared the disapproval of his co-workers if he stayed on the job. So he avoided making a decision but finally went out on strike. The strike dragged on for weeks, and when his bills began to pile up, he got a job for evenings and Saturdays, working as a watchman. To get this job, he had to lie and tell the personnel manager that he sought a permanent job. This went against his moral grain, and he felt guilty. However, he had a mortgage to pay and a wife and two kids to feed, so he bit his lip when he fabricated his story, then worried incessantly about how embarrassed he would feel if discovered. He believed he had done a wrong act and damned himself because of it.

The strike ended, and Joe went back to his regular job. He could not bring himself to resign the part-time watchman job, however, because he thought his new boss liked him so much. Meanwhile, his golf cronies tried to get him on the course on Sundays, and since he did good carpentry, his friends asked him to do favors for them by building or repairing furniture and cabinets. He could not turn down the golf invitations, and because many of the people who asked him to do carpentry had done him favors in the past, he found himself unable to turn down their requests. Soon all his time got filled, and his wife felt increasingly angry about his absences. When she threatened to divorce him, he started to have anxiety attacks over what to do to satisfy everyone. He felt so nervous he thought he soon would go crazy, and he began to fall farther and farther behind on his projects as he worried about what to do.

Faced with a myriad of incomplete tasks, and desperate, he attended a Workshop on Overcoming Procrastination at the Institute for Rational Living in New York City. During the workshop, he revealed that he thought he *must* get all the work (and golfing!) done, *must* satisfy everybody, and *must* condemn himself for his inability to schedule everything properly.

I (W.K.) and Joe's workshop group showed him that his main problems stemmed from his perfectionistic and love-need attitudes and that better scheduling would not help those. We helped Joe see what he kept doing to himself and got him to ask whether his predictions of doom would come true if he quit his watchman job and canceled some of his carpentry projects. We also helped him see how he created his anxiety attacks by trying to maintain others' approval at all costs. And that he didn't rate as a weak or rotten person for his actions, but merely as a person with some pretty nutty ideas about having his *musts* and the procrastinating to which they led.

Joe decided to quit his part-time job, to spend more time with his family, and to do other things he wanted to do for himself. With considerable apprehension, he embarked upon these assignments and later reported that none of the "horrible" consequences he expected materialized. In fact, his friends supported his plan to scale down his activities and his part-time employer easily accepted his resignation and wished him good luck. Meanwhile, his relationship with his wife improved dramatically, as she felt immensely pleased with the change he had made in altering his destructive life style.

Certainly this didn't end all of Joe's problems. No one workshop can produce a miracle. It did, however, provide Joe with an approach to dealing with his irrational assumptions about needing people's approval in order to accept himself. He also saw that approval can provide pleasure—but hardly when you sacrifice everything to attain it. He learned how his perfectionistic leanings interfered with his living, and upon returning to his home environment felt more tolerant and understanding of himself.

Anxiety and Procrastination

Anxiety usually results from anticipating future pains, believing you can't cope with them, and awfulizing about them. In awfulizing, you tell yourself your plight would prove terrible, horrible, or catastrophic. Thus, while failing a test, losing an arm, growing old, or picking the wrong career could bring great unpleasantness and inconvenience, your awfulizing over such eventualities represents an overgeneralization which almost certainly will result in depression, anxiety, and other "awful" feelings.

When you awfulize, you take truly unfortunate conditions, such as learning that you have cancer or that a dear friend has died, and escalate them over and above sadness and grief to the point of your virtual immobility. Your catastrophic thinking then greatly augments your distress.

If you create extreme anxiety because you anticipate and awfulize about a poor outcome, you easily can throw yourself into a panic and fear going crazy. You will not, in all probability, go crazy, but you will make yourself additionally anxious about this—hence more panicked. Because of your double-headed panic, you may then procrastinate about or completely withdraw from the activity you predict will have an "awful" outcome.

When you awfulize, you may pay an added penalty. Rather than experiencing great sorrow and strong unhappiness about, let us say, having heart trouble, you may raise your blood pressure by thinking your plight a monumental catastrophe. You thereby block enjoying the life you do have—and actually decrease your longevity. Although this may sound callous, if you really have only half the pie of life (because of something like heart trouble), you'd do better to savor that half than lament about the half you may miss.

What does awfulizing really mean? In essence, *awful* refers to the worst possible happening—something at least 100% bad. Practically nothing ever proves 100% obnoxious (even if you slowly get sliced to ribbons, you could get sliced *more* slowly.) But your devout *belief* in "awfulness" keeps you focused on what you miss and unfocused on the realities of what you *can* savor in life.

As a perfectionist, you will not want to take adventurous risks. You will think you *need* certainty and guarantees. These "needs" again encourage procrastination, as they lead to considerable indecisiveness. You seem unable to make up your mind about what you want, and you tend to stand pat and hate yourself for so doing. You may not feel able to choose a career, a mate, a meal, a suit or dress. You may then view your indecisiveness as *awful*, and suffer further bad consequences.

Sally's indecisiveness, for example, resulted in considerable anxiety and procrastination. She worked at a job she despised but showed up for work day after day for ten years in a state of anxiety and near-depression. She believed she could not leave her job, as she could not feel sure she would do better at some other position. Over the years, she had engaged in endless debates with herself about whether her age would prevent her from making a job switch, and, at twenty-nine, saw herself as over the hill.

She also wouldn't make up her mind about which of three males she wanted to marry, or about whether she'd better wait for one who might ultimately prove better for her. When she got together with her friends, she would practically never suggest that they do something *she* liked. Instead, she would follow their lead. That way, she wouldn't feel responsible if they made a poor decision. Her namby-pambyism and refusal to commit herself to anything but the status quo helped her hate herself when a project someone else suggested turned sour.

Sally's indecisiveness, stemming from her perception of herself as inadequate, resulted in considerable procrastination. While she did maintenance tasks promptly, she sank into a morass of inertia and despair in the rest of her life. Only after considerable rational-emotive therapy did she begin to make commitments and to follow through with them. In the process, she observed that others did not sulk if one of her choices for an activity turned out badly, that nothing awful happened when she took action on her own behalf and gained little by it, and that she could fully accept herself even when she failed to accomplish her objectives. She also discovered that life requires considerable risk-taking and that she took far deadlier risks when she compulsively tried to maintain an unhappy status quo.

Anxiety often derives from a presumed necessity for closure. The Gestalt psychologists, Wertheimer, Kohler, and Koffka, introduced the closure theme. According to this principle, humans tend to complete, or to close, tasks which they see as incomplete. Extending this concept, procrastinators may focus and ruminate on uncompleted tasks, strongly "need" to finish them, and nag themselves as long as the tasks remain undone. In the process, they often fail to do a project because they bog themselves down in their own nagging.

Zeigarnik proposed that we remember unfinished better than finished tasks. Procrastinators often prove his point. They tend to dwell upon incompleted projects, to worry over them, and to experience anxiety.

Some individuals, remembering incompleted tasks and craving closure, try to know everything possible prior to starting them. Naturally, more procrastination! Some illustrations may clarify this problem.

Cindy procrastinates about writing her term paper. She spends days at the library gathering articles and other resources, but dares not begin until she covers every possible source. She already has much more material than she can ever use, and feels overwhelmed, and she doesn't know how to integrate what she has.

George believes that, in order to cure his emotional problems, he has to know himself totally and not miss a single point in his psychotherapy sessions. He feels so anxious about missing the "crucial" statement that he tries to memorize everything his therapist says. He follows the same pattern on his job, where he tries to memorize everything his boss tells him about how to handle customers. As a result, he copes nicely with problems for which he has a ready-made formula, but makes himself anxious over most other contingencies because he doesn't completely know how he "should" handle them.

Knowledge represents power to George, and he sees gaps as fearsome powerlessness.

Wally, a psychotherapist, tape-records and takes copious notes on everything his clients tell him. He currently has enough notes to write a book on each client but functions poorly in his work. Rather than concentrate upon how his clients bother themselves and how he can show them how to stop doing so, he "has to" discover how every client statement fits into the theory he operates by. Needless to say, his clients get disgusted and leave.

Cindy, George, and Wally lose out in gaining perspective by trying too hard to bring closure to their tasks. The harder they run to get the big, "complete" picture, the more anxious they feel and the more they neglect other areas of their work.

How can you minimize anxiety? Mainly by vigorously and persistently disputing the irrational beliefs you hold that help you create it. One technique of doing this kind of disputing, we call DIBS—an acronym for Disputing Irrational Beliefs. In DIBS, you ask yourself a regular series of questions and actively dispute them, either on paper, on a tape recorder, or in your head.

Let's take Cindy's main irrational belief—that she must spend days in the library gathering resource material and that she dare not begin to write a term paper before she explores every possible source. Using the DIBS outline, she would question herself as follows:

CAN I RATIONALLY SUPPORT THE BELIEF THAT I MUST EXAMINE EVERY POSSIBLE SOURCE BEFORE I WRITE MY TERM PAPER? Answer: No, I can not.

WHAT EVIDENCE EXISTS OF THE FALSENESS OF THIS BELIEF? Answer: (1) I probably won't die if I write the paper without checking every possible source. (2) I can still, without checking all these sources, do a good paper. (3)

Other students manage to do good papers without compulsively reading every possible source. (4) No law of the universe states that I *have to* check all sources. (5) No evidence exists for *any* absolutistic *must*, including this one. I don't *have to* have anything,, including a perfect paper. (6) If I write my paper without checking every possible source, and it turns out less than perfect, I still probably will pass the course. (7) I won't amount to a totally rotten person if I submit a less-than-perfect paper—or even a bad one.

DOES ANY EVIDENCE EXIST OF THE TRUTH OF MY BELIEF THAT I MUST EXAMINE EVERY POSSIBLE SOURCE BEFORE I WRITE MY TERM PAPER? Answer: No, not that I know of. It might seem preferable if I examined these sources. But *preferable* doesn't mean necessary. And, actually, it probably would turn out *un*preferable if I covered all these sources, since I would consume too much time and energy in doing so, and other things in my life would suffer.

WHAT BAD THINGS COULD HAPPEN TO ME IF I DID THE PAPER WITHOUT EXAMINING EVERY POSSIBLE SOURCE? Answer: (1) I would do an imperfect paper. (2) I might possibly fail the course. (3) My teacher might not think highly of me. (4) If I failed the course and gained my teacher's disapproval, I might never get through school. (5) If I never got through school, I might have to give up the career I would like to follow. (6) If I gave up this career, I might gain less satisfaction and fewer monetary rewards. (7) Other unpleasant things might consequently occur in my life. (8) But if these things occurred, I would still only get inconvenienced in various ways. My life wouldn't turn out completely *awful, terrible* or *unbearable*. I could still live happily.

WHAT GOOD THINGS MIGHT HAPPEN OR COULD I MAKE HAPPEN IF I DID THE PAPER WITHOUT EXAMINING EVERY POSSIBLE SOURCE? Answer: (1) I could save a great deal of time and energy for other things. (2) I could do the paper quickly, instead of procrastinating about it. (3) I could impress my teacher in ways other than turning in a near-perfect paper. (4) I could overcome my compulsiveness about examining all these sources. (5) I could work at achieving happiness while working uncompulsively and turning in a reasonably good paper.

By actively disputing irrational beliefs that create your anxiety connected with procrastinating, you not only can help yourself surrender these beliefs—but eventually have an antiawfulizing philosophy that makes it difficult to have such beliefs in the first place, and relatively easy to give up when you realize that you have them.

Guilt or Shame

Feelings of guilt or shame contribute to procrastination in several different ways. For one thing, you can do something you consider wrong—e.g., copying your homework instead of doing it yourself—and condemn yourself so severely for this behavior that you depress yourself and consume time in self-downing. Losing this time, you may tend to procrastinate tasks that you might otherwise get around to doing.

For another thing, you may feel ashamed of the quality of the work you do—for example, the biology reports you turn in. Feeling this shame, and not wanting to experience the discomfort of doing other reports and bringing on such feelings again, you may hold back from doing them—in fact, put them off forever.

Shame particularly occurs in regard to procrastination itself. Gertrude bothers herself when she leaves on a short vacation. She dwells on the work she leaves undone and believes that she doesn't deserve to enjoy herself because she hasn't finished it. By damning herself for her "wrong" behavior, she makes herself feel ashamed and guilty. With these feelings, not only do her incomplete tasks remain undone, but she ruins her vacations. Clearly she accomplishes little by feeling guilty.

Tying her value as a person to what she does (and doesn't!) and defining her behavior as unforgivable do not help Gertrude change her ways. Indeed, by bogging herself down with guilt, she actually works less efficiently. As with Maude, when Gertrude forgoes her vacation to "catch up," she still fritters away many hours and accomplishes little because she spends time and energy downing herself for her goofing and also resentfully balks at spending her vacation working.

A better plan? Well, if you do procrastinate, give up shame and guilt (self-downing) about your dallying—particularly if you contemplate a vacation or other pleasurable pursuits. If shame (and other forms of self-hate) prevented procrastination, this behavior would hardly exist! If so, instead of writing a book on overcoming procrastination based upon a philosophy of self-acceptance, we might well tell you how to make yourself guiltier and more self-hating.

To rid yourself of efficiency-robbing feelings of shame and guilt, try to break the chain of thoughts creating these feelings. You can do this by identifying the various irrational themes involved in guilt, and by disputing each of these. Two frequent themes or concepts consist of: (1) "I did a wrong thing by procrastinating" and (2) "I therefore rate as a lousy person." The first proposition sometimes proves false, when questioned, since you *can* tarry for good reasons (e.g., fatigue or more important things to do). The second proposition has virtually no validity. Even if your procrastinating has no saving graces, how does it follow that you rate as a totally wicked or no-good person for dallying? A person who acts lousily *now*, yes. But a rotten person for all time? No!

Can you never experience legitimate feelings of shame and guilt? Not if you use the RET somewhat purist definition of these feelings. For it first includes a sense of your acting irresponsibly—I acted mistakenly, wrongly, or immorally, and I would like to act better in the future." RET highly endorses this acknowledgment of irresponsibility or wrongdoing. It holds that, along with your fellow humans, you have decided to live in a social group and abide by the social contract that group espouses—by its moral standards, rules, and laws. Consequently, when you fail to do so, you had better realistically admit your shortcomings and resolve that, in the future, you will do your best to behave morally instead of immorally.

But shame and guilt go beyond a sense of wrongdoing to a feeling of self-downing. In guilt, you tend to say to yourself, "Because I acted wrongly by needlessly harming others, I have a bad essence—a total rottenness." And in shame, you tend to say to yourself, "Because I acted wrongly by stupidly doing this or incompetently doing that, I have global stupidity or incompetence, and I will almost inevitably continue to act stupidly for the rest of my days." In both these cases, you don't merely acknowledge your bad deeds but your bad *self*. And, since your*self* or your ongoing *you-ness* consists of everything you have done, do now, and will do in the future, you cannot legitimately give it a global, conclusive rating or report card.

Moreover, when you down yourself, instead of merely observing your traits, performances, or other *aspects* of self, you really see this self as meriting damnation—as having the universe single it out for eternal punishment. You not only inaccurately appraise it in empirical terms (by comparing it to other human selves, who also appear globally unratable) but you magically devil-ify it—assume that demoniacal forces will keep it in mind forever and bring about for it only the miserable consequences that it "deserves."

Shame and guilt, then, constitute feelings that go far beyond feelings of irresponsibility and wrongdoing. Whereas the latter help you assess your crummy behavior and try to change it, the former get you to focus on your wormhood and louse-hood—which presumably remain unchanging. Again, as we keep emphasizing, feelings of shame, guilt, self-downing, and worthlessness *interfere* with your changing your ineffectual behavior and consume valuable time and energy that you might otherwise use to bring about such change.

So by all means make yourself acknowledge your procrastination and other errors. And try, as hard as you can, to correct and eliminate these errors. But don't waste any time flagellating yourself, your you-ness, for making mistakes. That merely leads to more of the same mishmash!

Depression

Feelings of depression frequently extend your feelings of shame and worthlessness to their illogical extreme: "Now that I have done so badly so many times, and seem to have the essence of badness in me, I realize I *can't* ever do any better. How hopeless! I might as well give up and do nothing." This combined belief in your badness and the hopelessness of your ever acting any way but badly almost certainly will depress you.

So will extreme feelings of low frustration tolerance and self-pity about the unpleasantries of life. In this respect, you generally tell yourself something like, "How horrible things seem! Not only does my present academic program look difficult, but next year's program looks as bad or worse. How hopeless! I'll *always* lead this dreary existence." Again: feelings of depression lurk right around the corner if you keep up this kind of thing long enough.

When you feel depressed, particularly through a combination of self-denigration and low frustration tolerance, you can easily resort to procrastination. You tend to think, "What good does it do for me to keep trying? I won't succeed at anything—regardless of what kind of work I do. So why bother? I might just as well put it off." Feeling depressed, you tend to see yourself as overwhelmed by mountains of work and experience great helplessness in doing it. You don't believe you can mobilize yourself and may disparage yourself all the more. Because: "I can't seem to stimulate myself into action." Result? Further procrastination!

Overcoming depression involves thinking and acting against the irrational thoughts that cause it. You can examine each irrational theme: What evidence exists for your belief about life's hopelessness? Or your belief that positive changes cannot alter your current course? How does procrastinating at making changes render you a helpless, worthless human? Why can't you *stand* (not why don't you *like*) your present situation?

In addition to vigorous self-questioning, you can powerfully disrupt depression with activity. By forcing yourself to work actively you can overcome both procrastination and depressed feelings about it. This does not mean that the process, though simple, proves easy. It doesn't. You'll often find it quite hard—but *ultimately* rewarding.

As Paul Hauck and Aaron T. Beck have shown, depression involves several complex elements. You vigorously blame yourself, pity yourself, and often focus as well on pitying others. In all these aspects, you insist that not only do you find things bad but they must not stay that bad. You *have* to do better. The conditions of the world *should* improve for you. The people you care about *must* not have serious afflictions.

These powerful *musts* seem an intrinsic part of the human situation—few among us do not believe in them much of the time. And just because we find others subscribing to them, we believe them all the more true. Bosh! Whatever miserable conditions beset you and your loved ones, these conditions often exist—and that remains that. Would that they didn't! Would that things got much better! But they often don't. When you fully accept that grim but inescapable fact and when you actively work to do what you can (and forget what you cannot) to make conditions better, then *and then only* you may banish depression. How about accepting *that* challenge?

Psychological Set and the Self-Fulfilling Prophecy

Psychological set involves your tendency to respond in a particular and predictable fashion. Your response, however, depends upon a variety of factors, including current motivational state and past habits. Numerous studies show that a person motivated by hunger generally will "see" food in ambiguous and rapidly exposed pictorial stimuli, and a sex-deprived individual may "see" sexual symbolism in the same stimuli. Your dominant motivational state, therefore, often shapes your "perceptions."

Because of your habitual avoidance of certain tasks, you may have a predisposition or "set" to view them as burdensome, and to view yourself as unable to accomplish them. Unthinkingly, you continue to repeat patterns of behavior that in the past have helped you procrastinate.

If you have a set or tendency to view yourself as a "goofer," you may divert yourself into less productive and worthwhile tasks, or try to avoid work altogether. Often you obsess about trying to live life the "easy" way. All too often, however, this "easy" way turns out unsatisfying.

As a student, you may spend so little time studying that you barely get through school, or, indeed, do not. You then have a set that life must have no hassles, and you distress yourself when the going begins to get rough. As an effective strategy for overcoming this problem, you not only can question the irrational belief, "Life should prove easy," but can force yourself into action until you set a precedent for more efficient and effective behavior.

At times, you so strongly have a set to fail that you almost assure failure. For example, Randi would often find it difficult to fall asleep, especially after a troublesome day or when she looked forward excitedly to some special event the following day. Believing a good night's sleep important and fearing she might not get one, she would panic around bedtime by repeating to herself, "How awful if I remain awake tonight!" Naturally, she would remain awake most of the night, and rise the following morning, tired and agitated.

She also would create a self-fulfilling prophecy in social situations by telling herself, "I *have* to make a good first impression." Believing she had to appear friendly and articulate, she made herself so tense that she appeared distant and aloof. Because of her attitude about past failures, she feared failing each new time, and tried to compensate by insisting that she had to succeed *this* time. What happened? She remained so tensely self-absorbed that she looked even more distant and aloof—fulfilling her prophecy once again.

Summary

Emotional disturbances seem as plentiful as spring rains. They come in many shapes and sizes, and include perfectionism, the dire need for love, anxiety, shame and guilt, and depression. Although all these kinds of disturbed feelings exist in their own right, they also tend to get combined with procrastination and avoidance.

Fortunately, practically all forms of serious disturbance have clearcut cognitive components, and directly stem from a devout belief in certain *shoulds* and *musts*. Fortunately, too, you can fairly easily discover these absolutistic demands and commands, once you look for them within the RET framework. The cognitive solution to procrastination-linked disturbance, therefore, largely involves looking actively for the irrational decrees that you place on yourself and others, defining them as clearly as you can, and vigorously and repetitively undermining them until you have much less of a tendency to use them again.

You probably won't, if you resort to rational-emotive analysis and reconstruction, overcome all your tendencies toward disturbance and never feel emotionally overwhelmed or (underwhelmed) again. But you may come surprisingly close to this goal!

8. Behavioral Methods of Overcoming Procrastination

Because rational-emotive therapy comprises a comprehensive system that includes cognitive, emotive, and behavioral aspects, and because it employs all three of these facets of psychotherapy quite consciously, some people view classical behavior therapy—as, say, practiced by the followers of B.F. Skinner and Joseph Wolpe—as a subheading under the general heading of RET. In some respects, this seems correct. RET almost always utilizes behavioral homework assignments and includes, at times, virtually all the techniques—such as desensitization, assertion training, and operant conditioning—that behavior therapy employs.

Viewed in a nonclassical and more modern sense, however, behavior therapy includes all kinds of cognitive and emotive methods, as such authorities as Alberti and Emmons, Cyril Franks, Goldfried and Davison, Kanfer and Goldstein, Arnold A. Lazarus, Michael Mahoney, and Rimm and Masters have shown. I (A.E.), Donald Meichenbaum, Aaron T. Beck, and other behavior-oriented therapists have used the term *cognitive behavior therapy* to describe a special kind of "broad spectrum" behavioral approach that includes philosophic, informational, and persuasive elements; and one can easily argue that virtually all "behavior therapy" practiced today really falls under this cognitive-behavior classification. If so, RET comprises one of the most important forms of cognitive-behavior therapy and, whether acknowledged or not, intrudes itself into the work of innumerable practitioners of behavioral methods. Most of the leading behavior therapy institutes in the United States and Canada consciously employ RET along with other modalities, and frequently see that their clients read the RET literature, expecially *A New Guide to Rational Living* by Albert Ellis and Robert A. Harper.

RET includes behavioral, activity-directed homework assignments not merely because they work but because they constitute an integral part of rational-emotive theory. For the theory holds that humans talk themselves *and* act themselves into self-defeating life patterns. Thus, you convince yourself that you not only find addressing your public speaking class difficult but *too* difficult and anxiety-producing and that you cannot *stand* doing it. So you put off doing that just as long as you possibly can, and you somehow manage to get through the class with a minimum of talks.

As you procrastinate in this fashion, largely as a result of your *beliefs* about the horror of speaking poorly, your delaying *behavior* reinforces a training and ideational process that significantly helps you to accentuate your terror of public speaking and to increase your avoiding tendencies. For, practically every time you actively hold yourself from speaking before the class, you *also* do several other negative things, such as: (1) strengthen the *habit* of nonspeaking instead of that of speaking; (2) *practice* avoidance rather than classroom involvement; (3) avoid acquiring the training and skills that you otherwise would get if you spoke and spoke and spoke: (4) strongly indoctrinate yourself, over and over again, with beliefs about the horror of speaking.

Note, in particular, this last point—the understanding of which looms as exceptionally important in overcoming almost all avoidant habits. Just as active participation in anything tends to give you favorable attitudes toward that thing, inactivity helps you acquire unfavorable attitudes toward it. When you force yourself to speak up in class, you tend to bring up or reinforce such ideas as, "See—I *can* speak up. I haven't dropped dead by doing so. I thought I would fail completely, but I didn't do that badly. In some respects, I even did well. You know, maybe if I kept doing this, I would even learn to speak up and not feel anxious about my classroom participations."

Conversely, avoiding speaking in class will tend to help you—and often *most* powerfully—to think as follows: "If I had spoken up and failed to do well, I *would* have found it awful. Speaking up, or even thinking about speaking up, in class *does* constitute a horror. I can see that I *have* to feel terribly anxious about speaking. I *never* will feel comfortable about it, or even have the ability to speak up at all. Now that I have avoided speaking up, and feel relatively calm, I can only sensibly keep avoiding it forever." Or, you may conclude, "See! I avoided speaking up and I knew I weakly gave in to my anxiety feelings. How horrible of me to do so! That just proves how incompetently I behave. How can an incompetent like me *ever* conquer a difficult task like speaking up in class?"

Because action goes with thinking, both influencing it and getting significantly influenced by it, RET—which takes a truly interactional or transactional view of human functioning and malfunctioning—holds that humans rarely cure themselves of their "emotional" hang-ups unless they specifically, concretely, vigorously, and persistently act, move, and propel themselves in counterattacking directions. If you want to overcome your superstition about black cats, you'd better, in addition to *convincing yourself* that they can't really harm you, *approach* a number of black cats. If you want to eliminate your anger at, say, your Aunt Matilda, you not only had better prove to yourself that she *does* have the right, as a fallible human person, to act the way she often does, but had better keep in contact with her, give her a chance to prove how obnoxiously she behaves, and *then* show yourself that you *can* stand it, and that you don't *have* to anger yourself at her, and that you need *not* find her an *awful person* just because she acts badly.

Behavioral actions, then, greatly help you to give up your nutty ideas. If you have an enormous fear of talking to strangers and you force yourself, time and again, to talk to them, you'll have great difficulty in retaining this fear—in believing that they will all hate you, harm you, or cause some disaster to happen to you. You will also counteract your irrational beliefs that you can't talk to them at all, that you can never talk to them well, that you have to stutter and stammer each time you address them, and that you can never gain any skill in conversation. These ideas persist largely because you *refuse* to test them in practice. As soon as you do test them, they tend to fade away or at least to grow dimmer.

Moreover, forcing yourself to speak to strangers when you enormously fear doing so constitutes evidence that you have given up this superstition. And forcing yourself to study regularly or to write a paper on time provides evidence that you definitely *can* do these acts. All the self-propagandization in the world—"I know I can do it; it won't kill me to do the studying or to write the paper"—will not convince you thoroughly until you actually *do* these things. Once you do them you have evidence that you really *can*; while when you merely say "I know I can," you merely have evidence that you *think* you can.

In ridding yourself of procrastination, therefore, or at least in significantly minimizing your tendencies to surrender to it, activity homework assignments loom as important, almost necessary. In this chapter we shall show you how you can map out and effectuate these kinds of assignments.

Behavioral homework assignments come in two varieties: activity and intellectual assignments. Actually, the two go together but one may have a special emphasis. Suppose you want a new job but procrastinate about going for interviews. Your homework assignment to yourself may simply consist of setting a goal of a minimum number of interviews per week—say, five—and of making sure you go on at least this number. If you carried out this assignment, you not only would stop procrastinating (an activity or *in*activity process) but would also tend to work against your irrational *ideas* about having interviews.

Thus, you may believe that (1) you do poorly at interviews, (2) you can't stand your ineptness in this connection, (3) you may do poorly at the new job, in case you get it, (4) you have to feel ashamed if you do poorly at it, (5) you can't stand the inconveniences of arranging and having the job interviews, etc. Merely by forcing yourself to go through with five interviews each week, you may automatically or unconsciously challenge these hypotheses and radically change them.

Better yet, you can also give yourself cognitive homework assignments, to ensure your doing this kind of challenging, which you can do consciously, *while* you carry out the behavioral assignments of having the interviews. Thus, you can dispute your irrational ideas every day by asking yourself: "What evidence exists that I *have to* do poorly on job interviews? Suppose I do act ineptly in that regard, how does that make me an incompetent *person*? *Must* I really do badly on a new job if I get one? Even if I do, what makes my performance *shameful*? Assuming that going for interviews has distinct inconveniences, why can't I stand the disadvantages involved in this process?"

If you set yourself *both* these homework goals, working against your inactivity *and* the ideas you use to bolster it, you will probably find it easier to get into action and easier to give up the crazy ideas. RET, as ever, involves cognitive *and* behavioral disputing; and often you can best do this double-headed kind of disputing by giving yourself definite, specific homework assignments, and by doing them on a daily or near-daily basis.

You can effectively apply RET concepts by taking a highly active approach to problem-solving, rather than by waiting for a miracle. Insight alone usually doesn't lead to behavioral change; and changing your act tends to lead only to limited philosophic understanding and modification of your irrational beliefs. Procrastination, in particular, involves highly rehearsed habits; to disrupt them radically, and bring them to an almost nonexistent state, you'd better practice, practice, and practice their opposites.

Reinforcement Principles

The basic principles of reinforcement, especially as applied to personality change and to the modification of self-defeating habits, stem largely from the ideas of the behaviorists, ranging from John B. Watson to B. F. Skinner. In recent years, a host of advocates of behavior modification have published data showing the effectiveness of these procedures—including Albert Bandura, C. B. Ferster, Hans J. Eysenck, Cyril Franks, Arnold A. Lazarus, Donald Meichenbaum, and Joseph Wolpe. These and other authorities have also espoused the use of behavior-modification procedures in self-management. Leaders in this area have included Marvin R. Goldfried and Gerald Davison, Frederick H. Kanfer and Arnold P. Goldstein, Michael J. Mahoney and C. E. Thoresen, Maxie C. Maultsby, Jr., Richard B. Stuart and B. Davis, and D. L. Watson and R. G. Tharp.

Skinner's theory of reinforcement or operant conditioning states that when you experience rewards or reinforcements after you have done a certain act, you tend to continue to do that act; and when you no longer get rewarded for doing it, you tend to stop performing it. David Premack and Lloyd Homme have added to this view the observation that you can utilize almost any act that you consider highly rewarding as a reward or incentive for performing almost any act that you think considerably less rewarding.

This means that if you procrastinate at, say, studying and you receive immediate rewards—such as lolling in the sun, listening to pleasant music, or feeling relatively unanxious—along with this procrastination, you will tend to continue to delay doing what you have promised yourself to do. But if all such rewards get withdrawn—and procrastination leads to no real satisfactions and perhaps only to boredom—you will tend to stop delaying.

Also, even if you feel rewarded for procrastinating but you feel more rewarded, say, by conversing with your friends, you may stop postponing things if you make conversing with your friends contingent upon doing them. Thus, you can contract with yourself: "I'll only allow myself to converse with my friends *after* I study for at least an hour every day." Knowing you will only allow yourself to obtain the reinforcement of conversing with your friends after an hour's study, you then will enhance the probability of your studying—though you could, of course, deliberately refuse to study and merely forego the reward; or else you could refuse to study and also refuse to forego the reinforcement. But operant conditioning or reinforcement works mainly statistically: It increases your chances of doing x, an arduous or unenjoyable but still desirable task, if you make the performing of it contingent upon y, an enjoyable (and usually unarduous) task.

Operant conditioning (sometimes called contingency management) can lead to good results with some simple planning on your part. Take virtually any task that you foolishly keep postponing, and ask yourself, "What do I like to do, really enjoy doing, that I do practically every day of the week?" Your answer could include things like having sex, talking to your friends, listening to music, reading the newspaper, smoking after a meal, or something else you particularly enjoy.

After selecting this enjoyment, contract with yourself, and do so definitely and with no nonsense about it, to keep doing the postponed project a minimum number of times or length of time each day and *only* reinforcing or rewarding yourself with the enjoyable thing *after* you have worked on the project Make sure you really *don't* reward or reinforce yourself until you have done what you promised yourself you would do on the project. No excuses! No task completed, no reward. And, if necessary, get a confederate—a roommate, a woman friend or man friend, a relative—to help you refrain from obtaining the reward unless and until you complete the project.

If you apply it steadily, this kind of reinforcement will not only get you to stop procrastinating, it will get you to *want* to stop. For if you *know* that you will get rewarded *only* after you do something, you will automatically, in many instances, begin to want to do that thing. You will often, in fact, look forward to doing it—instead of, as you now do, looking forward to not doing it.

Penalties and Aversive Conditioning

Shall you employ penalties as well as rewards to condition yourself to stop procrastinating or to do anything else you would find it better to do? We would say yes, in spite of the fact that some psychological literature says no. We say yes largely because of our clinical experience. Perhaps "normal" or unusually healthy individuals change their behavior and surrender defeating and longstanding habit patterns simply as a result of steady reinforcement. Perhaps. But our experience indicates that disturbed individuals, particularly those who have maintained a certain kind of disturbed behavior for a long period of time, rate as what we call D.C.'s—difficult customers. And *these* people frequently require, in addition to reinforcements for doing disciplined things, distinct and sometimes severe penalties when they fail to do them.

The procrastinating therapist who talked to me (A.E.) at one of my public workshops provided one of my favorite case histories. Although he did therapy himself and helped many individuals give up habits of procrastination, overeating, and other forms of undisciplined behavior, he rarely came on time for appointments (including those with his clients), and kept getting into difficulty with his wife, his children, his friends, and others with whom he came into steady contact. "What can I do?" he asked.

"Have you tried reinforcing yourself when you come early and failing to get the reinforcement when you don't?" I asked.

"Yes, but it doesn't work. I don't find anything I can think of that reinforcing."

"How about exacting severe penalties if you come late to any appointment?"

"Oh, I couldn't do that!"

"Why couldn't you?"

"I just wouldn't enact it. I wouldn't follow up."

"Okay then—suffer."

"What do you mean?"

"I mean that if you won't penalize yourself, won't bring on distinct pain immediately, every time you let yourself come late, then you'll almost certainly forever continue to come late. Which pain do you want—the pain of the immediate penalty (which you won't suffer if you do come early) or the pain of coming late and getting into various kinds of trouble forever?"

"Mmm," he said. "You mean I have no other choice?"

"Well, do you—really?"

"Mmm. Maybe not."

"Most assuredly not, as far as I can see. Now, what would you find really penalizing that you could use to get over your lateness problem?"

"I, uh, really can't think of anything!"

"Crap! You certainly can think of something. How about sending fifty dollars to a cause you hate, such as the Ku Klux Klan, every single time you come late? Or spending an afternoon with someone you dislike—say, your in-laws? Or cleaning the house for at least two hours?"

"Oh. I see what you mean. I hate to clean the house. That would probably do it."

"Well?"

"Uh, I—"

"Well!"

He finally agreed, with me and with himself, to clean the house every time he came even a minute late for an appointment. He wrote me a couple of months later that he had slipped only twice in this period of time; had swiftly seen, after cleaning the house, that he'd better arrive on time for future appointments; and now seemed to come early just about all the time. Aversive conditioning had really worked!

It normally does—if you enforce it. If you won't, it shows that you will stubbornly refuse to *work* at changing your ways—and that practically nothing will help you until you do. Keep waiting for magic, if you will. Lots of luck!

The Profit-Penalty System

A special kind of behavioral contracting that you can make with yourself in trying to overcome procrastination consists of the profit-penalty system. This involves using both a reinforcement and a penalty to help you with your problem. Thus, suppose you want to complete a thesis that you keep dallying on. You can break it down into relatively small parts—such as five pages of finished text—and can reward yourself by seeing an exciting movie or play, listening to get yourself "stuck" in a cycle of activity. Who knows, even five pages.

Or you can make the reward, usually a large one, contingent on your finishing the entire thesis. Thus, you can arrange for a trip to Europe or purchase a new wardrobe after you have completed the thesis.

At the same time, you *also* can penalize yourself for noncompletion. You can force yourself to eat an unappetizing meal every single time you finish less than, say, five pages of the thesis per day. Or, if the entire project remains incomplete by, say, December 31, you can donate a thousand dollars to a political party you loathe.

Again, you may use confederates to help you with your rewards and penalties. Thus, if you allow yourself to go to a good play only after you have finished twenty pages of the thesis, you can purchase the tickets to the play, give them to a friend with instructions to give them back to you on the day of the play, *providing* that you come up with the twenty completed pages. Or if you contract to donate a thousand dollars to a political group you loathe if you don't finish the thesis by December 31, you can put the thousand dollars (in cash!) in an envelope addressed to this group and have your friend mail it on December 31 if you do not show up with the completed manuscript by that date.

The Double-Profit System of Rewards

In using a variation on the profit-penalty system, you can make a no-lose agreement with yourself. Thus, if you have a report due on Friday, you can contract with yourself to have it finished—or else to pay your bills, which you may normally procrastinate about paying, on that day. Similarly, if you want to give up excessive eating and smoking, yet you keep procrastinating about both these tasks, you can agree with yourself that whenever you go over twelve hundred calories, you will not smoke the following day. This strategy often works surprisingly well, not only for weight reduction, but also for giving up smoking.

You can employ this procedure in a chaining fashion. That is, once your weight diminishes, you may try to reduce smoking by forcing yourself to work against another procrastination problem (such as putting off studying) every time you go over the quota of cigarettes you have set for yourself.

You can also use this approach for overcoming procrastination to set up a double-bind situation for yourself. You decide, say, to give up both smoking and excess eating simultaneously. Each day that you eat or smoke more than your agreed-upon quota, you reduce your other quota the following day. If you goof in both areas, you force yourself to complete another deferred task in addition to continuing to work on the eating and smoking problems.

Naturally, you can employ any combination of profit-penalty or double-profit techniques which appear helpful. You can use the profit-penalty plan, for example, by forcing yourself to write a complimentary letter to a disliked organization when you fail to maintain the double-profit plan.

Reminders

Written reminders sometimes can serve as an important aid in working on your problems. Three beneficial slogans include: "Doing gets it done," "Don't let the grass grow under your ass," and "Instead of all or none, why not take a bits-and-pieces approach?" You can make up cards with sayings like these and post them as reminders. Sometimes a small piece of tape or dot on a watch or thumb can serve the same purpose as the card: The tape or the dot symbolizes the phrase which reminds you to take the kind of action you desire. Tying strings around fingers and making and carrying lists also can help. Memory, as previously mentioned, often can use jogging. Trusting memory or hoping to do something later may prove unrealistic. If you don't do a task right away, write it down in a notebook, and read the entries daily.

The Bits-and-Pieces Approach

Doing things in bits and pieces may provide one of the best antiprocrastination techniques. Many who procrastinate let their daily tasks pile up until they have dozens of projects to do—all seemingly pressing and all necessary. They then tend to feel confused and indecisive as to priorities. Using the bits-and-pieces approach, you begin an important project and work away at it as long as feasible. For example, if you have not cleaned your house or apartment for several months, force yourself to do *some* cleaning. Don't put up with no cleaning at all!

Similarly, if you keep procrastinating on an exercise program because you believe you have to do the whole sequence of exercises every day, try to do at least a few of them, without insisting that you complete the whole series. Better to complete half the series than to do *no* exercises! No hard-and-set rule states that anything less than the whole sequence has no value whatever. At worst, what you do succeed in performing will prove partially effective.

If you keep putting off writing a book while waiting for large blocks of free time, why not write a page or two a day? At the end of the year, at that rate, you can finish three hundred and sixty-five to seven hundred and thirty pages, even if you never find any large blocks of time in which to do the writing.

By using the bits-and-pieces approach you whittle down incomplete tasks and finish large parts of projects (and eventually the entire project) on a limited basis. Of course, once you start a small part of a task and get into the swing of it, you may discover that you complete the entire operation—particularly if it doesn't take long to finish.

Riding the Wave of Inertia

Occasionally if you begin a task, such as writing a song, you can use the momentum you gain to switch over into another, perhaps onerous task—e.g., responding to correspondence. You may find the second writing task easier when you have built up a positive momentum for the former—because you already have started to use writing materials and may already have gotten yourself in the mood for writing at that time. Even if not in the mood, you may still find it easier than when you don't have the materials out and available.

Similarly, when you start cleaning your apartment, you may discover it easier to switch over to the long-postponed activity of throwing out old clothing. Your making a list of tasks to accomplish may help remind you what to do if you get yourself "stuck" in a cycle of activity. Who knows, even that long unwritten resumé may get finished that day!

The Five-Minute Plan

You can use this approach to start a wave of positive momentum. In the five-minute plan, you agree to start a project and to stay with it for at least five minutes. At the end of that time period, you ask yourself whether you will continue for another five minutes, and let your actions serve as an answer. Use this as a nondemand procedure. You don't *have* to work beyond the original time period. Like most people, however, you probably will find that inertia begins to build and swell once your five minutes of forcing yourself ends. So you can try another five minutes!

Do It When You Think of It

The concept of doing something just as soon as you think of it deserves serious consideration. Very often, you will put small tasks aside to do tomorrow or the next tomorrow. Your work then piles up, often gets mislaid, and looking for it among the rubble of disorganization amounts to quite a project. Not only does the work remain, but you then have the additional burden of having to refind it. If, instead, you get into a routine of handling paperwork, paying bills, returning phone calls, etc., *just as soon as you think of doing so*—and not one second later!—you avoid the problem of relocating the materials needed for such tasks and save considerable time and effort. Another useful variation of this method: If, say, you have an unpaid bill or unanswered letter, tend to it *as soon as you actually see it again* and *don't* put it back into an unsorted pile. Or put its due date on it in large crayoned letters, so that you vividly recall this date every time you come across this undone item.

Facing the Music

If you face the music by doing a delayed task, you generally get *less* rather than (as you falsely predict) *more* criticism and pain. Thus, if you procrastinate for a long period of time, your undone task prevents others from doing their jobs or inconveniences them in various ways. Not uncommonly, you then will feel reluctant to follow through out of fear of their asking, "Why the delay?" and your having to make up excuses. Generally, however, you had better face their annoyance than "eliminate" it by continued delay.

Jane went to a dinner party while her male friend waited at her apartment until she returned. When the time came for her to leave, she felt reluctant to inform her hostess that she had a date for that night and would have to leave early. So she stayed on and on . . . and on, waiting for an "appropriate" break in the conversation. After that, she procrastinated out of fear of (1) the disapproval of her friends when she told them that she had a date and (2) the horror of hearing her male friend's criticism when she showed up hours late for their date. So she stayed until the bitter end, anguishing all the while about what her friend would say when she finally walked in the door—if he had bothered to wait. She even considered sleeping over at a woman friend's house to avoid the confrontation, but decided to "bite the bullet" and take her medicine. She indeed had a rough time with her date—who already had gone to sleep at her apartment. But he forgave her, mainly because she honestly—finally!—faced the music.

In general, the more you put off a task which involves other people, the harder it seems to do it, because you additionally pressure yourself by believing that they will think badly of you, and that *that would prove horrible*. You'd far better think, "Those who suffer from my procrastinating may despise me, but I can see their reactions as *most unfortunate* instead of as horrible. Since I don't *want* their disapproval, I'd damned well better *stop* my stupid, and self-defeating delay!" This realistic and *non*-self-castigating outlook will help you end rather than help you continue putting things off. Even if you remain excessively late in completing a project, work at accepting yourself with your procrastination and not at psychologically beating yourself over the head for it. You thereby have more time and energy available to perform instead of consuming it flagellating yourself for nonperformance.

Establishing a Set Time for a Routine

Setting a precise time for doing something can help considerably. Often you will procrastinate because you lead a somewhat disorganized life; and establishing a realistic schedule may prove helpful. For example, forcing yourself to exercise first thing in the morning (or the last thing at night) could result in the exercise process taking place more or less habitually once you set it up as an established routine.

Rather than organizing work according to priorities, and leaving it in different piles to do at a later time, force yourself to start one of the priority tasks as soon as you do the organizing. Keep at the work, perhaps by using a bits-and-pieces approach. Try to allow reasonable amounts of time in which to complete each activity. If the task consists of details which you view as unpleasant, do at least part of the job, rather than run off to do something more interesting. In fact, try to hold out an enjoyable task as a reward for completing the less-interesting one.

Try to avoid spending much time making out schedules you probably won't use. A client, Sam, continually planned his work, but generally didn't follow through on his plan. He maintained a routine of planning rather than of doing. He solved this problem by forcing himself to do certain tasks at specified times so as to get himself into a routine of acting rather than procrastinating.

Modifying the Environment

Your atmosphere or "working environment" can contribute significantly to studying and writing procrastination. Many students persevere at not studying in their bedrooms by conveniently making available to themselves a bed to fall asleep or masturbate on or a stereo, radio, or TV set with which to divert themselves. A typical bedroom environment has a large number of cues which stimulate thoughts about behaviors other than studying or writing!

While some persons can work productively under almost any environmental contingencies because of a prepotent task orientation, the majority of humans in our culture do not seem to fall into that category. So, if you easily divert yourself from producing in a particular environment, why not try to change that setting? Instead of preparing to take tests and writing term papers in your bedroom, go to the den. Or better yet, truck yourself off to the library! In all probability you will find fewer distractions there and have a greater tendency to work.

Some individuals work better in a quiet atmosphere, some with music playing in the background, some with others working nearby, and some in isolation. Whatever atmosphere seems most productive for you, try to create or find that work-facilitating environment.

Playing the Probabilities

Persons who procrastinate in creative areas often wait for the moment of inspiration to overtake them before they begin to work. Meanwhile, they gain additional practice in procrastinating.

Instead of putting off writing, sculpting, painting, why not use probability theory to help you begin? For when you *un*spontaneously force yourself to begin a project, you stand a good chance that you will *sometimes* stumble into a streak of *spontaneous* brilliance and produce a surprisingly great product. The more you produce, even by premeditatedly plugging and chugging away, the greater the probability that you will turn out some unusually appealing work.

This also hold true for nonprocrastination in meeting new friends or lovers. If you wait till you feel totally inspired to make such contacts, you may go out to make them three or four times a year—and fail miserably because of the small sample of people you will meet. If, taking advantage of probability theory instead, you uninspiredly force yourself out to look for new friends at least once a week, you will tend to meet scores of people, and spontaneously to act so well with at least *some* of them that you probably will end this playing-the-probabilities year with more intimate associates than you have time to handle!

The technique of playing the probabilities also gives you highly useful experience and practice. If, as an artist, you have no great inspirations, but you nevertheless force yourself to keep drawing or painting, you may get inspired as you work. But even if you don't, the mediocre art you create probably will improve your craftsmanship—so that when you finally do come up with an inspired conception, you will more likely have the ability to execute it. With social contacts, too: the more you uninspiredly and steadily force yourself to make them, the more communication skill you normally will acquire—so that when an outstanding candidate for friendship or love finally comes your way, you will stand a better chance of gaining this person's attention and approval.

Self-Monitors and Reminders

Behavior-modification investigators have found that reinforcements and penalties do not have to consist of "real" satisfiers (such as love, money, or food) or of "real" deprivations (such as forfeiting love or money or performing some painful task). They also can include "symbolic" or invented rewards and disadvantages. If you procrastinate about shopping for food, you can penalize yourself tangibly by purchasing groceries you don't like and you can reward yourself when you shop promptly by purchasing some ice cream or other tasty foods.

But you can also deal with your problem intangibly or symbolically by keeping track of the number of times you procrastinate about shopping and marking these times on a conspicuous calendar, or posting a chart of your procrastinating behavior on your bathroom mirror. This kind of reminder or monitoring device itself often will prove reinforcing or penalizing. For if you note, after a few weeks, that your chart shows continual procrastination, you will tend to feel displeased with your behavior, to keep it more graphically in mind, to note its disadvantageousness, and to minimize it. And if your chart shows a notable decrease in self-defeating delaying, you will tend to feel pleased with your habits, to note their advantages, and to continue them.

You also may make yourself ego-involved with you record of procrastinating and nonprocrastinating by rating yourself *as a person* with regard to it. Thus, you may say to yourself, "Because I keep procrastinating, I rate as a pretty worthless individual," or "Because I procrastinate less, I now feel more worthwhile." This kind of ego-involvement has advantages—since it may motivate you to do better in order to accept or respect yourself. But it also has enormous handicaps—since you tend to preoccupy yourself with it, to down yourself, to believe that a rotten person like you *can't* change, and thereby to motivate yourself to give up and continue to act badly. We therefore do *not* recommend this kind of motivator.

But if you can stick with, "Because I have stopped my foolish putting things off, I feel good about this, and now know that I can enjoy myself more!" you begin to accept *it*, your behavior, as good and not *yourself*, the doer of the behavior, as a great or noble person. Then, at worst, if you later fail, you can see your acts as lacking, rather than see yourself as worthless for performing poor acts. If you stay with rating your doings, you can feel happy when you do well and sad when you do poorly. If you jump to rating yourself, you take too much of an emotional risk. You then tend to interfere with the changing of your behaviors.

As George Ainslie has shown in a fine review of the literature, "Specious Reward: A Behavioral Theory of Impulsiveness and Impulse Control," we have a strong human tendency to go for the pleasure of the moment—what he calls the specious reward—rather than for the "real" or the longer-term rewards of the future. We often choose, therefore, a desired object (e.g., a cigarette) that we find immediately available rather than a *more* desired object (e.g., better health) that we only can get by deferring or foregoing immediate pleasure. Rats and other animals also seem to act similarly to humans in this respect.

Realizing this fact, and wanting to give up specious or minor rewards for more important ones, we can invent certain tricks, or precommitting devices, to make the immediate specious rewards unavailable or undesirable; or we can direct our attention away from the cues that signal the availability of these rewards. This means that, if you enjoy immediate rest and tend to choose it over immediate work that will result in greater gains (such as finishing a project to get a good mark in a course, or at least to pass the course and get a degree), you can arrange things so that (1) you make immediate rest impossible (e.g., you force yourself to go to a library to work on the project), (2) you make rest undesirable (by setting a timer that repeatedly interrupts it or by agreeing with yourself that if you rest you will forego some other pleasure that day), or you deliberately refuse to focus on the desirability of resting (e.g., keep your mind steadily focused on something else, such as the approval you will get from your friends and your teacher if you complete the project quickly).

Your ability to predict the future—which Myles Friedman calls the essence of rational behavior—can help you make side bets and arrangements to control your short-range hedonism. You can make these side bets in a public manner—tell your friends, for instance, that you will complete the project (and not only thereby fail to get their approval but bring on their greater disapproval if you don't). Or you can make them entirely private, in your own head, and approve of your own behavior if you "win," disapprove if you "lose." In fact, you can make this kind of private side betting a kind of end in itself, a game that gives you enjoyment in its own right. You then can focus so strongly on it that you make it an important part of your existence.

You have a strong, probably innate tendency to make up side bets and to get distinct pleasure or pain from their outcomes. For example, you often decide that one team rather than another will win at baseball or tennis, and you mentally "bet" on this team. If it wins, you feel happy with your "bet" and if it loses you feel disappointed. No money actually changes hands, and you may even oppose actual gambling. But your side-betting in your head focuses your attention on the game, on the particular team you have chosen to "bet" on, and (probably most important of all) on your ability to "bet" successfully.

In stopping your procrastinating, you can use this side-betting tendency to good effect. You can mentally "bet" that if you stay home to work on the assigned project, you will give yourself a score of ten; and if you don't work on the project, you will give yourself a score of zero. You can set a total of 100 points as the "winning" goal and give yourself ten days in which to reach it. You also can give yourself a "bonus" of twenty-five or fifty points in case you do attain this goal in the ten days' time; and you can accept an "anti-bonus" of no points, twenty-five points, or fifty points in case you attain it in thirty days, twenty days, or fifteen days. You can invent all kinds of variations on this side-betting scheme.

If you engage in these kinds of side bets (either privately in your own head or with the knowledge of your friends), you first of all tend to focus on the betting, and on the challenge of winning it, instead of on the immediate satisfaction of resting. And this very kind of concentration frequently helps you use long-range instead of short-range goal-setting.

Second, you thereby invent for yourself other satisfactions—the pleasure of winning the side bets—than the mere pleasure of gaining the specious goal of immediate rest. You easily can make these satisfactions much more important to yourself than those of quick gain.

Third, you tend to remove or overcome the other specious satisfactions that you give yourself by rebelling against completing projects on time. Thus, when you agree to finish a project in ten days, you may invent a rebellious kind of false integrity in *not* completing it. You then tell yourself something like, "I wouldn't have agreed—since I really don't *want* to do it—but would have arranged to complete it later or even not to do it at all. Since I acted weakly, I now have to act strongly, to prove to people I agreed with that they can't exploit me like this and make me into a ninny. I'll show them! I'll deliberately finish the project late, to let them know what fine integrity and strength I really have!"

This kind of false integrity frequently interferes with your unargumentatively finishing a project, even if you have agreed to do it. When you make side-betting an effective motive, you can overcome false integrity by making it *more* important to you to win one side bet (e.g., that you will do the project in ten days and gain the 100 points you have set up in your head as a "bonus" for completing it) than another imaginary side bet (e.g., winning the "fight" with the people who have taken advantage of your "weakness" and presumably forced you against your will to accept the doing of the project).

In many ways, then, you can use monitoring and side-betting to help you achieve rewards or reinforcements for doing a project on time that significantly add to the intrinsic reward of completing the project itself. As a human, you tend to side-bet anyway; and much of your procrastination results from your ineffectual and stupid internalized betting. Why not look at this side-betting process and use it effectively for your best, instead of your worst, ends?

Reminder Files

Make your appointment book, desk calendar, or special large filing book into a reminder file. Suppose you have a tax form to fill out by April 15. You place the form (or a notation about it) in your appointment book—yes, right there, in the book itself—on, say, Monday, April 14. Make sure you fill it out when you look at your appointments that day, come hell or high water! If, foolishly, you don't, put the tax form (or notation about it) back into your appointment book on the page for Tuesday, April 15, Wednesday, April 16, Thursday, April 17, etc. Do this *every single day*, until you fill out and pay the tax form. Will this kind of tickler system make your appointment book untidy? Good! You can always tidy it up by paying your tax bills on time—or in advance!

The Use of Confederates

In addition to using confederates to help you enforce any program of reinforcement or penalty that you set up for yourself in regard to overcoming procrastination, you also can use them in the actual performance of delayed tasks. If you refuse to get down to studying, you can make an appointment with a friend who doesn't have this kind of difficulty and study with this person. If you delay in going for a passport or a tennis permit, you can arrange to go for it with a friend who also wants a passport or a permit, or who will merely agree to accompany you.

In using confederates, you increase the probability of doing a task promptly for several reasons: (1) You will tend to feel obligated to keep your appointment with your friend or classmate, because you will inconvenience this individual if you do not keep it. (2) You may not want the disapproval of your confederate if you avoid the appointment or fail to keep to the project for which the two of you set it up. (3) You can choose a confederate who has little difficulty getting down to work and who will tend to serve as a good model for you. (4) Vexing activities that you do with others frequently take on a much less vexing quality, and sometimes you actually enjoy them. (5) If you have difficulty getting around to something because of your fear of failing at it, the presence of a confederate may increase the probability of your succeeding or may help reduce your anxiety about failing.

We find this last point especially applicable to some of the risk-taking and shame-attacking homework assignments that we give during our group therapy or marathon procedures at the Institute for Advanced Study in Rational Psychotherapy in New York. Thus, if we give one person the assignment of going out on the street to speak to a stranger, he or she frequently returns to the group and reports a failure to carry out the assignment. But if we give the same assignment to two people, and one merely watches while the other carries it out, and then the first person watches while the second person carries it out, we find them both more likely to do the assignment.

So don't hesitate to use confederates sometimes. Not always though! For if you train yourself to study *only* when someone else studies with you, you limit yourself and "confirm" the view that you can study only under these conditions. By all means, when you seriously procrastinate, make use of confederates or associates to force yourself to get to work. But also experiment with doing the same activity by yourself, without the necessity of having someone else around to do it with.

Expect Backsliding

Procrastination habit patterns have built up over the years, and even with the most determined effort, you occasionally will slip back into old patterns. When this happens, don't think you have lost everything. It merely means that you have imperfections, like all other humans. Furthermore, if you believe you have lost everything when you slip, you fail to put your problem clearly in perspective, and overlook recent gains you may have made.

Wanda, for example, had successfully kept to her diet for six weeks. One day she arrived for her counseling session noticeably upset. She had gone on a food binge the night before, she explained, and, "It blew my diet."

When I (W.K.) pointed out to her that she had stuck to dieting for one hundred and twenty-five meals, and only once had she feasted excessively, she responded, "I never thought of it that way. I only saw my failing." When I asked, "What stops you from resuming the diet at the next meal?" she thought a moment and, much relieved, said, "You know, I can't find any reason not to."

Wanda had momentarily lost *perspective* because of what she told herself: "How awful to have failed myself in keeping up with my diet! It seems all over!" She had enveloped herself so much in her own disappointment and anxiety that she didn't see she had taken but one step backward for 125 steps she had taken forward. She saw herself as hopelessly backsliding, because she perfectionistically believed that she had to keep 100% on her diet. Anything less amounted to a complete failure. She didn't view it as better to do a worthwhile task part way then to avoid it completely. Even if Wanda dieted only half the time, she would still do 50% better than not dieting at all.

Wanda has the same problem as many others. She views her world in a pessimistic way. Instead of seeing the bottle as nearly 100% full, she chooses to focus on its less-than-1% emptiness. Instead of acknowledging her percentage of progress, she high-lights her imperfections. This perspective often proves most unsatisfactory, reduces motivation for dieting (or for any similarly difficult discipline) and tends to lead to more, rather than less, procrastination.

Summary

To a large extent, needless and foolish procrastination stems from low frustration tolerance—from your viewing getting down to work on a task as *too* hard and your insisting to yourself, consciously or unconsciously, that you will benefit more from delaying than from completing it. You go, as humans frequently do, for immediate gratification rather than for long-range hedonism. You make side bets in your head that you can get away with delay—when you most likely cannot. You therefore obtain a specious rather than a real set of rewards for your postponements.

Knowing this, and having an ability to predict future behavior and future payoffs, you can deliberately establish another kind of reinforcement and penalizing system which effectively counteracts the ineffectual one that you keep employing.

You can do this behaviorally by literally reinforcing yourself with some satisfier that you personally enjoy soon after you do an arduous task instead of procrastinating at it; and you can actively penalize yourself with something you abhor immediately after you procrastinate. If you give some thought to setting such reinforcements and penalties, and to carrying them out come hell or high water, you will interfere seriously with your procrastinating and in all probability overcome it.

You often can achieve the same effect without utilizing actual reinforcements and penalties, by making side bets in your head, by rewarding yourself with a system of points or scores, and by penalizing yourself in a similar fashion. Such side bets, particularly if they do not lead ultimately to behavioral rewards and penalties, may ultimately prove useless. But they do have a helpful quality and you may use them to good effect, as long as you do not tend to put your ego, or rating of your entire person, on the line. You literally or figuratively can arrange things so that you like or dislike *it* when you do things on time or procrastinate. But don't magically and dangerously jump into liking or disliking *you* for these behaviors!

9. Emotive Methods of Overcoming Procrastination

Although usually seen as a highly cognitive and behavioral method of psychotherapy, RET also includes a pronounced emotive component. Most especially, RET therapists give their clients what Carl Rogers calls unconditional positive regard, or full acceptance. They do not condemn these clients for literally anything they do (although they often may disapprove of the clients' behavior and help them to try to change *that*); and they show them how to accept themselves completely, even though they continue to behave badly. RET therapists also put clients through a good many emotive, evocative, dramatic exercises—such as our famous shame-attacking exercises—in order to help them change their basic self-defeating philosophies and act more appropriately.

Some of the emotive-evocative techniques of RET do not easily adapt to self-help procedures, but many of them do. In this chapter, we shall outline how you can utilize certain RET emotive methods with regard to procrastination problems.

Forceful Self-Persuasiveness

RET theory holds that emotions, for the most part, stem from (though in their effects go physiologically beyond) strong or biased thinking. If you say to yourself, moderately or weakly, "I think I don't like studying very much; no, I guess I don't," you probably will have a mild emotional feeling of dislike when you think about or engage yourself in studying. But if you vehemently think, "I definitely don't like studying! I really loathe it! It makes me sick just to think about it!" you will tend to feel exceptionally emotional about it, and may therefore find your studying actions blocked.

The problem remains: How do you ameliorate or change your negative emotions about engaging in some unliked project? Answer: by *strongly* fighting against and determinedly surrendering these negative, and especially your negative, *must*urbatory, attitudes about this project.

Take, for example, one of your main *musts* that may encourage you to procrastinate about reading the sizable amount of material that your English Literature class requires: "This work seems *too* much to do. The class *must* not include so much reading! How unfair!"

Vigorously and forcefully keep attacking these foolish ideas with statements such as: "Nothing amounts to *too* much work—only much!" "The class *must* include an enormous amount of reading—because it *does*!" "So my professor acts unfairly! No reason whatever why he must act fairly!" "No matter how obnoxious this reading appears, I definitely *can* do it. And I'd better!" "So I find the goddamned reading annoying! What hand has writ that conditions *must* not annoy me?"

Again, your resistance to doing assigned reading probably includes another, self-downing set of *shoulds* and *musts:* "I cannot possibly read all this material and know it well—as I must! I *should* have the ability to read it more quickly and retain it easily! What makes those bastards give me so much stuff to read when I rate as a *schnook* who only barely can get by with this kind of material?"

Again, vigorously and powerfully you try to drum into your head, until you truly believe them, counter-attacking ideas like these: "I damned well *can* read all this material, even if I never do it very well!" "I don't *have* to read it perfectly!" "No reason exists why I should have the ability to read it more quickly and retain it easily!" "No one rates as a bastard—even my English professor!" "If I have difficulty with the reading, that never makes me a *schnook*—at worst only an individual who acts *schnookily* in this particular area." "If I fail, I fail! It won't kill me!"

Shame-Attacking Exercise

Although procrastination frequently stems from low frustration tolerance, it sometimes also follows shame or self-downing. If you feel terribly ashamed of doing poorly at, say, bookkeeping, you may keep putting off making out tax forms, balancing your checkbook, or doing your accounting homework. As an antidote to such feelings of shame, you can practice the RET exercises of deliberately doing "shameful" things until you inure yourself to them and see that nothing sensational happens in regard to your doing them.

You can, in this connection, make yourself fill out your tax form—and then have it checked by a certified public accountant, who can point out your errors to you. Or you can take a noncredit course in bookkeeping or banking, knowing that you probably will do poorly in it. Or you can deliberately give one of your friends a check that bounces, to show him or her that you do not keep track of your checking account very well.

The shame-attacking exercises you do can relate specifically to your procrastination hang-up—like those we list in the previous paragraph—or they can constitute unrelated risks or shames. Thus, you can deliberately go around with a painted face, looking like an American Indian. Or you can go to a formal affair in an informal outfit. Or you can stop people on the street to tell them, "You know, I just got out of a mental hospital."

If you do enough of these general shame-attacking exercises, you will keep showing yourself that you *can* survive, that if people think you silly they *won't* bite you or kill you, and that you have given enormous and specious importance to many things which really have relatively little significance. By contradicting your self-shaming philosophies in these ways, you acquire a global outlook that helps you ultimately feel that *nothing* really proves utterly shameful, even though many things have their distinct handicaps. With this kind of outlook, you will find yourself much less prone to procrastinate about many things whose performance you previously would have viewed as highly embarrassing or humiliating.

Authentic Self-Disclosure

As Sidney Jourard has shown, you tend to create and to hang on to shame-creating philosophies when you hide from others, only show them your "impressive" side, and refuse to disclose many presumably disgraceful things about yourself. As we previously noted, inactivity or refusal to do something tends to propagandize you into believing "It *would* prove horrible if I did this!" And nondisclosure of your "horrible" failings makes you think and feel that they really rate as "horrendous."

Procrastination, of course, frequently includes a nondisclosing element. You greatly fear that people will see how awkwardly you act in public, so you postpone going out or you go out and sit on the sidelines. You feel horrified about the possibility of a member of the other sex discovering that you have had little dating experience, so you procrastinate about going to social affairs or about arranging dates when you do go.

The antidote? Some amount of ruthless disclosure. Say to people when you go out in public, "You know, I haven't had much experience speaking in groups, and I fear I'll do poorly." Confess to the member of the other sex you would like to talk with at a social affair, "I don't feel comfortable talking to you right now, because I haven't done much of this kind of thing before, but I would like to get the practice!"

Open up. Disclose yourself. Take more risks. Of course, you'll often do poorly. Of course, you'll fail to achieve the goal you want. But at least you'll practice, at least you'll learn. And the next time, and the time after that, will tend to seem easier and better.

Role-Playing

Role-playing probably goes back to the earliest historical times, but it has a more recent origin in the field of psychotherapy in the work of J. L. Moreno, Raymond Corsini, Fritz Perls, and other proponents of psychodrama and allied techniques. Under the name of behavior rehearsal it also has gained popularity among behavior therapists.

Although we use role-playing in RET and have a therapist direct you in certain aspects of it, you also can utilize it with your friends and acquaintances. Suppose you hesitate about going for job interviews because you feel terribly afraid that you will acquit yourself poorly. To help yourself, you merely have a friend act as the job interviewer—play the role of a rough interviewer who tries to put you on the spot . . . perhaps rattle you. You do the best you can, playing yourself in this kind of performance; and then your friend (perhaps with others) gives you a critique of what you did well and badly. You then rehearse the scene, to see whether you can do better—and perhaps do it several times until you have acquired more "interviewing" skill.

Suppose, again, you procrastinate about speaking up in class, and even avoid going to class for fear that the teacher will force you to recite. You role-play speaking up in class with a friend or a group of friends—and have them tell you how you performed.

You also can reverse roles, in both the job interviewing and the classroom reciting experiences—you play the interviewer or you play the teacher and let one of your friends play the interviewee or the pupil. You can then see, perhaps more objectively, what constitutes good and bad performances. You may also acquire some insight into and empathy for the role of the person who normally interviews you or asks you to recite in class.

By this kind of role-playing, you can begin literally to act and "feel" your way into dreaded situations, to acquire more skill at them, and thereby to overcome much of your dread. Then you will tend to procrastinate less about them.

Expressing Feelings

One of the most used of all emotive methods of therapy consists of catharsis or abreaction—letting your feelings out as much as you can, and sometimes, as in abreaction, living out feelings from your past that you presumably have held in or repressed over the years. Freud at first used this technique a great deal, but then realized that it didn't produce especially good results. Many other therapists—including Gestalt, Reichian, and primal therapy—have continued to use it, again with questionable results. Not that it doesn't help the individual to express his or her feelings adequately, and sometimes to get temporary relief from "blowing off steam." But the questions remain: Does this do more than temporary good? Doesn't it often do more harm than good, in that such feelings as anger get practiced and reinforced by expression? For, as you tell someone off, angrily push him away, or savagely beat a pillow that you imagine represents his head, don't you reinforce the belief with which you make yourself angry—"He *shouldn't* have done that to me, that lousy son-of-a-gun! I hope he drops dead!"

RET tends to resolve this dilemma by encouraging people to express their appropriate rather than their inappropriate feelings. Thus, if you feel displeased about someone's behavior and you wish to express that feeling to this person, you *assert yourself* and constructively try to get him or her to change the behavior. For your displeasure, we can assume, usually constitutes an appropriate feeling, and you had better do something to try to get your annoyer to stop displeasing you in the future.

Anger or rage, however, almost always amounts to an inappropriate feeling, in that it follows from your *demanding*, not merely *wanting*, another to stop behaving in an obnoxious manner, and from your denigrating this person, in toto, rather than his or her acts. Consequently, in expressing anger you act *aggressively* rather than *assertively;* and as Alberti and Emmons, Arthur Lange, Patricia Jakubowski, and other therapists have shown, while you may well follow the healthy goal of assertion, you'd better not follow the unhealthy one of aggression. RET strongly concurs.

If, then, your procrastination stems from a lack of assertiveness or from the fear of expressing your genuine displeasure with others' acts, you can sometimes assertively practice expressing yourself, thereby eliminating a prime reason for procrastinating. Suppose you have had enough of your roommate's talkativeness and want to study. You feel afraid, however, to offend her and to tell her frankly that you have other things to do. So you postpone studying, and spend perhaps another hour or more listening to her. You may then hate yourself for remaining so passive, and wind up by hating her for "making" you listen to her.

In instances like these, you can force yourself—yes, literally force yourself—to assert yourself. You can tell her directly that you have had enough of her talking, thus expressing your feelings of displeasure. Or you can merely tell her that you have other things to do, risk her disliking you for breaking away, and start your studying.

Again, if your partner keeps coming late to lab, never seems prepared to do the experiments you have to do together, and cops out on his appointments with you to write up the experiments, you can passively and unassertively let his behavior go by—and therefore delay getting in your lab reports. Or you can force yourself to express your displeasure and concern, and risk his hating your guts.

In general, as in the shame-attacking exercises discussed previously in this chapter, you can practice expressing yourself to many people on many occasions—one, by telling them what you don't like about their behavior and two, by refusing to do what they want you to do. Even though this kind of expressiveness may have nothing directly to do with your procrastinating, if you get in the habit of acting this assertively, it probably will hold you in good stead in regard to other forms of nonassertion which may interfere with your doing projects promptly.

Again—don't confuse assertion with aggression! And don't think that you *have to* assert yourself about all your feelings! As long as you acknowledge how you really feel, and get rid of your inappropriate feelings (especially rage), you then can decide whether you find it worthwhile expressing some of the feelings you have. If you dislike a friend's behavior, you may easily tell her about your feeling and risk the loss of her friendship. But if this same person supervises you on a good job that you want to keep, you may wisely decide to feel displeased with her behavior but to keep your feelings to yourself—at least until you can find another job!

Similarly with professors. By all means acknowledge that you feel highly annoyed at the lack of clarity of your math teacher. Acknowledge this, if you will, to yourself, to your classmates, and even to certain school authorities. But don't convince yourself that this professor *must* teach better, and don't enrage yourself about her not doing what she "must." Once you can, without rage, feel annoyed at her teaching, you have a *choice* as to whether or not to tell her about your annoyance. You may decide to risk it in some cases, consider it highly unwise in others. If you feel appropriately displeased at her *teaching* rather than inappropriately angry at *her*, you can sanely choose whether or not to express your feelings And once you de-anger yourself at her for teaching so badly, you will tend to take away your motives for violently rebelling against her by procrastinating about doing your math.

Rational-Emotive Imagery

In RET, we often use rational-emotive imagery as a method of attacking an emotional problem, including one concerned with procrastination. Suppose that you just won't get around to keeping your room in order, and you continually put off cleaning it. You know it looks like a mess and you know that its messiness interferes with your efficient functioning but you keep putting off tidying it up.

To do rational-emotive imagery, a technique originated by Dr. Maxie C. Maultsby, Jr., and modified by Albert Ellis so that it includes more elements of implosive therapy or flooding, you first imagine yourself continually procrastinating about cleaning your place, and vividly see it as a complete mess. Everything seems disordered and you cannot function at all because of the disorder. As you intensely imagine this scene, and your still failing to do anything about it, you let yourself experience what feelings you would spontaneously or naturally experience. You will usually find that you feel depressed, anxious, or self-downing. Let us suppose you do feel depressed and self-denigrating.

Let yourself fully acknowledge and get in touch with these feelings. Don't allow yourself to avoid them. Then, after you keenly feel them, you make an effort to change them—yes, change the way you feel in your gut—to feelings of sorrow, regret, or disappointment but *not* of depression or self-downing. Let yourself feel—in fact, *make* yourself feel—*only* quite sorry and disappointed about your behavior, but not depressed or self-deprecating. You may not think that you can change your feelings when you want to do so, but you can. We find exceptionally few individuals who, within a few minutes of working at it, cannot bring about a radical change in their feelings. So persist till you *do* change them.

Once you no longer feel depressed but only regretful about not keeping your room in order, and about getting bad consequences because of your procrastinating, observe *how* you have made this change. What have you done to create it? What have you now told yourself that a few minutes ago you did not believe? Look at what goes on in your head as you change your feelings.

Normally, you will have told yourself something like, "Okay, so I let my room get untidy and sabotaged myself because of this unnecessary disorder. How regrettable that I have done this! But not more than that. The world won't come to an end. I can fix this later, and even if I never do, I don't have to see myself as entirely rotten. I still remain the same person before I messed up the room so badly. What a pain in the neck! Now let me see what I can do to correct this deplorable situation."

When you see what you have done, what you have begun to tell yourself, in order to change your feeling from self-downing to disappointment with your acts, practice vigorously and persistently having this new set of beliefs and feeling these new feelings. Spend at least ten minutes a day for the next several weeks imagining yourself procrastinating about your room, getting poor results, and acknowledging your failing in this respect. Then let yourself feel, first, the inappropriate feelings of depression and self-downing—and a little later, the appropriate feelings of sorrow and regret about your delaying cleaning the room. Continue this practice until, whenever you think about and intensely imagine your self-defeating behavior, you deplore it but accept yourself, and automatically feel, therefore, only disappointed, not depressed.

At the same time, or perhaps some days later, you can start working on your low frustration tolerance itself, rather than on downing yourself for having it. Thus, this time you imagine your room very messy and continuing to get messier day by day. Then imagine your having to clean and tidy it—and your having to do so in a thoroughgoing manner. Somebody or some set of events forces you, against your will, to clean the room and to keep it very tidy every day. No matter how you try to wriggle out of this, you have to do the cleaning and tidying.

As you intensely imagine this scene, let yourself again spontaneously feel what you would feel if it actually occurred—probably anger, resentment, or self-pity. Let yourself acknowledge and get in touch with these feelings. Feel them!

Now, once again, with the same negative scene in mind, make yourself change your feelings to those of *only* frustration and annoyance, and *not* of anger and self-pity. Yes, no anger, no self-pity, but only frustration and annoyance. Keep at it until you succeed in doing so—which normally will take only a minute or two.

After you have made yourself feel only frustrated and annoyed, see what you have done, what you have told yourself to bring about this new result. Probably something like, "Oh, well—so I have to clean up the room. Too damned bad! I certainly will never like them forcing me to do this, especially on a steady basis. But I won't die of it! It only remains a hassle, not a horror. Tough! I'd better do it, if I can only get what I want this way, and not make such a federal case out of it!"

When you see what you have done to change your inappropriate feelings of anger and self-pity to the appropriate ones of frustration and annoyance, continue to repeat this process, again for at least ten minutes a day every day (including Saturday and Sunday!) for the next few weeks—until you spontaneously and automatically begin to feel irritated and annoyed rather than angry and self-pitying and until your low frustration tolerance begins to significantly decrease.

Rational-emotive imagery, as you can see, constitutes a therapeutic method that starts with a cognitive process (imagining), enables you to get deeply in touch with your feelings, includes changing your feelings (which you have much more ability to do than you normally realize), investigates the thoughts you employ in order to change these feelings, gets you to behaviorally practice a new set of ideas and emotions, and winds up by helping you acquire a distinctly modified philosophy about frustrating conditions and your failure to react well to such conditions. Although a simple exercise that takes only a few minutes a day, it has important cognitive, emotive, and behavioral components and consequently proves very effective in many instances.

Achieving Your Human Potential

You procrastinate, in many instances, because you consider doing certain things like writing a thesis onerous and un-pleasurable, and feel that they usurp the relatively little time you have for more satisfying pursuits. To some extent, you perceive correctly—since you will find many tasks unappetiz-ing, even though the results of doing them may seem benefi-cial. And you do have a limited life span and can cram only so many things into a normal twenty-four-hour day.

You may best solve this practical problem by trying to ar-range for the unpleasant things you do to lead to pleasurable results and by increasing the satisfying things in your life so that you don't mind the unsatisfying things so much. In both these respects, you can give considerable thought and practice to increasing your human potential—to finding more short-term and long-term joys that will significantly improve your life.

This involves a self-pushing and experimental attitude. First of all, you get yourself fully to accept the idea that you have a *right* to happiness and to make this your main goal. You live because you live—and you probably can't find any *special* reason, any cosmic purpose that the universe foists upon you, for your existence. You may invent such a pur-pose, but you can't very well prove it. Consequently, you have every right to *make* your own basic goals and ideals, and to choose survival and happiness as your main purpose.

You also have the right to maximize your happiness and minimize your pain. When you procrastinate, most of the time you foolishly believe that you achieve maximum hap-piness (e.g., ease) and minimal pain (e.g., work and effort). But you normally don't! So you'd better try again—try to stop the foolish procrastinating and to achieve more of your potential for happiness. You have this right. Choose it!

Once you decide to achieve your potential for more pleasure and less pain, you can do so in an experimental, experiencing way. For you don't really know what you like until you try it—and compare it to other things that you don't like or like less. Take a biologically based pleasure, such as sexuality. You naturally and spontaneously feel aroused at times, and if you try a common practice, such as intercourse, you may come to orgasm. Fine! You learn this, and you thereafter seek out more intercourse and more orgasms.

But various hassles tend to intervene—such as finding a partner, helping to arouse that partner sexually, bringing that partner to climax, and trying new things—such as new positions of intercourse or oral-genital relations—that at first seem awkward or difficult. So you tend to procrastinate about getting started. Or you begin to have sex but delay getting around to the "difficult" aspects of it. Or you hesitate to have a heart-to-heart talk with your partner about what he or she really likes and doesn't like.

Because of procrastinating and avoiding, you hardly achieve your potential for sex pleasure. In fact, you often get nowhere near it—or take literally ten years to approach it. You block yourself with the usual procrastination-creating ideas, "If I fail at this new sex act or my partner dislikes me for trying it, I will rate as a horrible person! Moreover, I find it very hard to try something new sexually. And this kind of difficulty shouldn't exist!"

The old procrastinating nonsense! As we keep showing, you can actively, vigorously dispute this nonsense, and give it up—so that you finally believe, "Yes, I may fail at this new sex act. But that would make the failure, and not *me*, bad. Naturally I find it hard to do new sexual things. But life *does* have its difficulties. And I'll find it a hell of a lot harder if I don't take some chances and get going!"

As you tackle the irrational ideas that block you sexually, you free yourself to widen your range of enjoyments. But freeing yourself to do something does not comprise the actual doing of it. The next step includes forcing yourself to do it. In sex, once you feel free to try various kinds of intercourse and of noncoital pastimes, you experimentally force yourself to try one, then another, then still another path—until you discover some that truly satisfy you. Forcing yourself to try things, moreover, means getting yourself to try them often and persistently enough to see whether they will "take." For eating oysters a few times may get you nowhere but eating them ten or twenty times may help you develop a real taste for them.

So you experiment! You push yourself—yes, push yourself—into new pathways. You try sex with the lights on, in the afternoon instead of only during the evening, on a chair in addition to a bed, in the open air rather than just indoors, and with as many other variations as you imagine might prove interesting. Achieving your human potential, in this as well as in virtually any other area, involves testing, trying, toying with new and different approaches. Most of the experiments you throw yourself into may turn out dull or wasteful. But a few probably will work out well, and even those that don't, give you valuable information about what you *don't* like—about your *own* tastes and bents.

Achieving more of your potential and discovering pleasures that you hardly conceived or dared try before gives you something to *un*procrastinate about. For if you really like, say, oral sex and your partner enjoys it, too, you will spontaneously *want* to go to bed with him or her, and your postponing sex may easily go by the board.

Discovering new and greater enjoyments, moreover, often helps you with your general problem of procrastination. For one of the main reasons you do not study may consist of your not-so-crazy belief that your life really *has* few satisfactions and that therefore you don't want to take on a rather unsatisfying task like studying. And this very dearth of gratification may make mere avoidance of study *so* pleasurable that it easily wins out over sitting down with your textbooks. If, on the other hand, you push yourself to find a few truly enjoyable pursuits—sex, love, chess, dramatics, or what you will—you may look forward to engaging in them so much after poring over your texts that you do not find doing so *that* troublesome. People who feel madly in love frequently take such a healthy attitude toward other aspects of their life, including work, that they do that willingly and enjoyably, too. The same thing may occur if you adventurously and experimentally achieve a higher potential for general living.

Summary

You can change your emotional reactions by working hard at modifying your cognitive evaluations and your behaviors.

But you also can alter your cognitions and your actions by working at changing your emotions. You may not find it as easy to get a handle on your feelings, and to directly affect them, as you can do with your philosophies and behaviors. But you can achieve several things in this direction.

For one thing, you can persuade yourself forcefully—which includes vigorously and dramatically—that you don't *have to* procrastinate, that you don't turn into a *rotten person* for postponing important things, and that you *can* stand annoying tasks. Second, you actively engage in shame-attacking exercises that will help you surrender the ideas that people *must* like you and that you *have to* accomplish various projects perfectly. Third, you can deliberately push yourself to reveal some of your "horrible" traits and performances to others, until you clearly see and feel that you and they can accept you with your failings. Fourth, you can engage in dramatic role-playing to help yourself acquire certain skills and to take "dangerous" social risks. Fifth, you can get yourself to acknowledge and express your appropriate feelings of dislike and can make yourself behave assertively rather than aggressively. Sixth, you can use rational-emotive imagery to get in touch with your self-defeating feelings and to exchange them, by cognitive-emotive practice, for more appropriate emotions. Seventh, you can work at increasing your pleasures and achieving more of your human potential, so that you can spontaneously enjoy life more and take away some of your major reasons for procrastination.

With these kinds of emotive-evocative-dramatic methods, you can supplement the cognitive and behavioral techniques used in RET and can more effectively and enduringly procrastinate less. You then have a comprehensive approach to surrendering some of your worst habits and changing self-destructive aspects of your personality.

10. Impediments to Overcoming Procrastination

While you may have relatively little difficulty in overcoming some emotional problems, you often will find it most difficult to overcome procrastination. Why? Because you easily deceive yourself in regard to it, and consequently often avoid admitting that you do procrastinate or that you bring on distinct disbenefits by needlessly delaying projects and tasks. We shall now outline some of the main ways in which you tend to rationalize about procrastination, and show how to look at your self-deception and overcome it.

The Mañana Attitude

You can avoid dealing with almost any emotional problem by refusing to face it in the present and by scheduling it for future consideration. We call this belief—"I really don't have the time to do this today but I'll willingly and easily do it to-morrow"—the *mañana* attitude. Consider the cases of Alfredo and Anna.

Alfredo would like to audition for an acting part, but he fears failing and doesn't really want to make the necessary effort to develop his acting skill because he believes it too tough. He has a motive for mastery and success, but also has fear and low frustration tolerance, and so he acts against rather than toward his goal.

Anna has a conflict about beginning her doctoral dissertation in anthropology. She has struggled for years—studied, attended classes, passed examinations—and has one last obstacle. But she suddenly finds all sorts of pleasant routines to amuse herself with and avoid her dissertation. She takes long trips, throws elegant and highly popular parties, and gains expertise in selling women's lingerie. Meanwhile, her time limit on the dissertation approaches and two of the members on her committee (with whom she has the best rapport) soon will retire. She really wants her degree—she could teach college if she obtained it—but she fears she won't do an excellent enough job, and that her committee members will feel disappointed with her. In addition, unsure that she will do well, she experiences twinges of fear about teaching college on a full-time basis. She quickly turns those thoughts off by planning a Halloween party, or by thinking up new marketing strategies. More procrastination about her dissertation!

Alfredo, when he contemplates auditioning for an acting role, does not tell himself, "I feel afraid." After all, that would not match up to his masculine ideal. Imagine the great Alfredo afraid! Instead, he tells himself he has not properly prepared (a half-truth) and will need to practice some more *tomorrow* before he can even think about auditioning.

Anna more freely admits fear but loathes risking disapproval, and resists trying something she might do poorly. She never had a problem about her school courses, as she had a good memory and could regurgitate all the facts her professors wanted her to know. Unfortunately, she had little opportunity to engage in original thinking throughout her college career, and realizes she probably will not astonish the world with an unusually creative dissertation. So she avoids working at it and tells herself that she has deprived herself of so much fun and excitement by religiously working at her studies, lo these many years, and that she owes it to herself to have fun before she gets too old. So maybe after Thanksgiving she'll begin the thesis.

Alfredo and Anna tell themselves some, but hardly all, the truth about their procrastinating. Sure, more practice at acting would improve Alfredo's chances of getting a good part, but he stalls at getting such practice. Sure, Anna could nicely lead a more balanced existence and broaden her social life. However, she does not have to make this an either-or proposition. She could spend some time each day on her dissertation and some time on developing herself socially and having fun. At least she could if she didn't so greatly fear failing. Both Alfredo and Anna take the pressure off themselves by deceptively using half-truths and by promising to do better tomorrow.

College students often epitomize the *mañana* attitude. Jack had to take a final examination in his major. He dillydallied about studying his notes until the day before the test. When this day arrived, he decided to begin, but soon felt too tired to study and played basketball instead. Maybe after a vigorous game, he would be in the mood to study. Fatigued, he returned to his apartment and told himself he would set the alarm clock for 4:00 A.M. and commence studying then. When the alarm went off, he reset it for 6:00, and then again for 8:00. As a consequence of his taking the test without studying, he had so little knowledge of the material that he did poorly. With the *mañana* approach, he first put off studying for a few days, then later for a few hours.

The Contingent Mañana

Virginia kept falling farther and farther behind in her work in the office. She thought to herself, "As soon as my marital difficulties straighten out, I'll catch up." As the work piled up, she started an affair and thought that her energies had to go into this all-important adventure. Soon she began to excuse her delays on the job by telling herself that she couldn't work until she resolved what would happen between her and her lover. Would she divorce her husband, keep the affair going secretly as long as she could, or opt for an open marriage? By making her office work contingent upon nonrelated factors, she delayed, delayed, and delayed, until her employer threatened to fire her unless she improved her performance. At that point she went into a flurry of activity, caught up, and then slumped back into her usual routine of do-nothingism and fantasizing about finding a new job.

Virginia believed that, tomorrow, when her personal life straightened out, she would operate more effectively on her job. We call this variation of the *mañana* attitude the *contingent mañana*. It takes many forms.

Reginald wants to take karate lessons but believes he needs to get into better shape before starting. After six months of planning to start we find our hero still putting it off. Janet wishes to meet some interesting new men, but believes herself overweight and decides to lose ten pounds before embarking on her quest. As with Reginald, she delays working on her weight problem and consequently puts off meeting men. Both set up preconditions or contingencies. Reggie believes he can't do karate well unless he feels stronger, but also fears he won't do well even then. Janet believes she won't attract men unless she loses weight, but also fears rejection if she weighs less, because then she might get turned down because of her "personality" instead of her weight. By focusing on exercising or weight reduction, both individuals divert themselves from their basic problems—poor self-evaluation and low frustration tolerance.

Some procrastinators use the *mañana* attitude to take the pressure off by promising themselves that they work better without pressure, and that they'll get around to doing a task when they feel like doing it. Unfortunately, that time rarely arrives, because of inertia, habit patterns, and psychological set to act and behave in dallying ways. Nevertheless, they patiently wait for the moment of truth to overtake them when they spontaneously will knock off all the work they have piled up. Eventually, this tactic may result in at least some of the delayed projects evaporating. More often than not, however, the jobs remain, take more trouble to complete, and get very sloppily done.

When you wait for inspiration, or force yourself into action because you finally have to do it or risk losing a job, friend, or mate, you tend to dissipate your energies endlessly. You also tend to repeat this cycle, nag yourself about the steadily accumulating tasks, and pledge away your tomorrows to escape making an effort today. But your todays stay unpleasant, as the incomplete tasks loom in the background of your thoughts, sometimes coming to awareness at the most inopportune times, as when you undertake an important project and wish to feel calm, cool, and collected.

Ineffectiveness of the Mañana Attitude

You sometimes can dispel anxiety over not completing a project by making an affirmative decision to complete the work at some supposedly opportune time in the future. Thus, through using a *mañana* diversion, you purchase a stay of execution. This pattern crucially involves your *decision* to perform later. You then no longer feel weak and unable to mobilize yourself but can look optimistically to the future without doing anything in the present to increase the likelihood of that improvement's ever taking place.

The contingency *mañana* works in a similar way. By deciding to do an intervening task, you can divert yourself from working on a major project and promise yourself you will finish the project after following through on the preliminary task.

Your rationalization of waiting for a moment of inspiration also proves diverting because it hypothesizes some opportune time in the future to more affirmatively complete a task. This seems a reassuring but hardly very workable idea.

Often, even when you use the *mañana* attitude or one of its variations, you still have nagging thoughts about the incomplete projects, as you feel suspicious of your resolve to follow through with future plans, based upon the fate of similar unfulfilled self-promises.

In sum, the *mañana* attitude partly works, since it provides you with a "solution" for failing to perform today. "I will find it easier to do tomorrow." But you still can recall vividly the hundreds of New Year's-type resolutions you have made and the few you followed through on. You then tend to feel flooded with anxiety, depression, or self-anger over your past and present weaknesses.

Grasshopperism

We often tell children the story of the grasshopper and the ant with the intent of teaching a moral lesson: "You'd better work and save for a rainy day rather than fritter time and energies away in frivolous activities." While neither the ant nor the grasshopper seems a particularly appealing character, a compromise between their extreme behaviors might provide a balanced solution for most humans. In the story, the grasshopper fiddles his summer away, and when the winter winds began to roar, he starves. Many people act in grasshopper fashion. They labor under the illusion that they cannot ever regain pleasure lost. Thus, if they must choose between studying for a test or attending a fraternity party, our grasshopper-inclined students choose the latter—often telling themselves they will study better in the morning, after a relaxing, fun-filled evening, or that they will go out only for a little while, then resume studying. What harm could anyone find in that? Often, on the following day we find our now "hung over" student scurrying quickly to class to get to the test on time or calling up the professor and feigning illness in the hope of taking the exam under more favorable conditions.

Grasshopperism typically does not result in our having as much pleasure as our smiling green summertime friend would seem to have had, singing and dancing. Actually, if we followed grasshoppers under their leaves at night, we might find them worrying over the food supply for the future and wondering if they'll survive.

Ants do not have a very peachy existence either. Sure, they survive the winter, but if we follow them into their holes, we may hear them lamenting about all the fun they miss. They keep themselves so compulsively busy that they don't take time to enjoy opportunities to develop their other talents. Antism can prove quite dull!

Escapism and Procrastination

Leaning back against an old apple tree, you can experience great thoughts and turn them into fine actions. Newton, sitting under an apple tree, purportedly identified the law of gravity, and many other noted scientists, poets, and inventors attribute some of their key discoveries to allowing their fantasies to stretch in many directions.

Absorption in fantasy, however, can have negative effects. Take the school boy or girl who stares out the window, or blankly looks at a book while daydreaming of better things to come. Or the haggard housewife's dreaming of a supreme lover sweeping her out of the depths of despair, rescuing her from her daily bottle of gin. These individuals use fantasy as an escape from the pains of their daily existences, particularly when trapped in a pattern from which they see no escape. Walter Mitty used the magic of fantasy to escape from his daily trials and tribulations, and so does everybody, to one degree or another. When you dominantly rely upon fantasy, however, you typically accompany it with procrastination.

Andy had many many plans he wanted to implement during his lifetime. While going through school, he would distract himself from his studies in fanciful anticipation of wonderful events to come. As a consequence, he did so poorly in school that his ambition to study medicine went down the drain. And so he fantasized about having a paramedical profession while he worked after school as a plumbing supply clerk, distracting himself with his fantasies and often bollixing up the plumbing orders. As a consequence, his position with the company remained marginal.

Many persons, like Andy, live their lives vicariously through their fantasies. They reluctantly work to actualize their desires, since fantasy proves enjoyable, and implementation involves effort. They find it easier to imagine a career of glory. Gaining movie stardom readily gets "realized" and great fame "follows." They elect themselves as the benevolent president of the world, with just a little imagination.

Charlie had a fantasy of working as a super salesman of educational materials. He believed that because of his work as a teacher he could persuade large school boards, such as the New York City Board of Education, to purchase his company's products. With commissions from these sales he saw himself acquiring a huge mansion atop a hill overlooking a green, pine-studded valley, where his wife, children, and pets could enjoy the good life in a pollution-free atmosphere.

He revealed this fantasy scene during one of his therapy sessions, swelling up with pride as though it amounted to an accomplished reality. Indeed, as he had knowledge and capability, he conceivably could make some major sales if he set his mind and efforts in that direction. He determined to contact some educational supply firms to see if he couldn't sell their line on a part-time basis, with the ultimate aim of doing it full-time.

The following week, a depressed Charlie arrived for his session. He whined that he had let himself and his family down by making no attempt to seek or apply for sales positions. Exploration revealed that he tremendously feared his fantasies would not work out and that he refused to make any effort unless guaranteed magnificent success.

Eventually Charlie's therapy group persuaded him to try selling and to discover whether he had talent in this area. As it turned out, he did, but not as much as he had dreamed of. However, growing surer of his competence, he added considerably to his income, and thoroughly *enjoyed* the two extra hours he spent selling after school. As an added dividend, he discovered that talking to new people enabled him to bring back more interesting things to talk about with his wife, and his relationship with her improved.

Entertainism

Hollywood, television, and magazines play upon people's fantasies by portraying persons who appear to have immensely satisfying and exciting lives. These adventures enable viewers psychologically to escape their problems by identifying with some of the heroes or heroines portrayed on the silver screen or the "boob tube." In lieu of striking out on their own to achieve the kinds of experiences they would like to have, they let their lives drift by as they watch what others do.

The Hollywood adventure more often than not portrays an

overly idealized person or aspect of life—the prepetually happy family. Even though the spectators realize the idealization displayed, they still may wish to model their behaviors after the ideals. Absorption in this pursuit may aid in fueling fantasies and promote further drifting from the world of planful action.

Numerous children, adolescents, and adults turn off to education because they do not find it sufficiently entertaining. Used to fast action, the TV watchers of the world look for rapid changes in their own lives. They see the classroom as too slow, its actions and learning as not rapid enough. Many school populations cultivate impatience as their trademarks. Even education majors find excitement not in the doing, but in the viewing. They desire knowledge to funnel in through a magical osmotic process from machine to person or from person to person, with little intervening effort.

Impulsiveness and Escapism

Various media encourage escapism through fantasy. We can not easily determine whether the media have shaped the appetites of Americans for greater ease and less tolerance for discomfort or whether they simply reflect the attitudes of the majority. Both probably hold true.

Impulsiveness generally stems from low frustration tolerance. Seeing a task as too tough or as not worth the effort (even though you desire the outcome), you may give up on it. You may then suddenly replace your inertia with impulsive bursts of frantic activity, when you grow weary of delaying gratification any longer and attempt to find rapid, impulsive shortcuts to obtaining what you want. Going all out and playing the horses to win "big" or trying to make quick kills on the stock market exemplifies this process in the economic domain. In the interpersonal area, a young couple may marry, not because they love each other, but as a way of leaving their overly restricting parents' homes. You may impulsively quit a job and run off to a different part of the country. Rather than deal directly with a problem, you may escape by fleeing and hope that, magically, your life will improve.

It generally won't! As a housewife who runs away to escape the drudgery of your daily routine, you usually will find a different drudgery wherever you go. While some kindly male may rescue you when you arrive at your new destination, you more likely will continue to experience the same pattern of difficulties as you did prior to leaving your family. If you deal poorly with problems in one environment you may easily transfer the same bag of difficulties into the next.

Impulsive bursts of energy directed at altering fundamental dissatisfactions in living typically don't resolve these dissatisfactions any more than waving a magic wand will set you free from psychological fears.

Escapism Through Drugs

When life seems too tough, some people turn toward artificial stimulants to disrupt boredom and to divert themselves from dealing with life's less happy elements. A man with an unsatisfactory view of himself may turn to alcohol to obtain euphoric refuge from the distresses and irritations of everyday living. A woman who won't tolerate frustration may "escape" through drugs, then use elaborate and "convincing" rationalizations for copping out on many problems: "We live in a crummy culture, so what difference does it make?" "Drugs will give me insight into myself." "I can quit any time I want to, but I prefer to 'get off' on drugs."

Drugging oneself into oblivion often appeals to procrastinating types. For people who procrastinate about acquiring good skills or daily about finding means of getting high on constructive aspects of life frequently feel they can get real kicks only from drugs.

Music and Reading as Escapism

Some persons spend considerable time listening to Bach or Mozart or old Beatles records—particularly when they have pressing tasks to complete. Suddenly taking an interest in a novel they have previously left to gather dust on a shelf, or feeling a strong urge to listen to records the night before a major test, they foolishly avoid the more important project. They rationalize this kind of substitution: "How unfair to deprive myself of the more cultured pleasures of life!" "After relaxing, I will attend to my studies better." Needless to say, such procrastinators often hardly read or listen to music at all, except when they feel some pressure to study for a test, paint an apartment, or some other unpleasant activity.

Overeating as Escapism

You easily may make yourself into a food addict when faced with a "distasteful" task or with failure. You cop out by running to the refrigerator or to the local ice cream parlor to avoid a problem. Later, you may hate yourself for weakly indulging your whims. With this kind of diversion you can deflect your attention from primary problems to additional secondary ones. Thus, you can damn yourself more severely for overeating to avoid failure than you would have condemned yourself for committing the failure you avoided.

Excessive smoking can work in the same diversionary way: First, you smoke to avoid doing reports; then worry about getting lung cancer and damn yourself for smoking; finally, divert yourself so "successfully" into this secondary worry as to make yourself procrastinate more about the reports. You can finish off by devil-ifying yourself for procrastinating!

The Cavalry to the Rescue

Many of the old cavalry movies contained scenes where natives—Indians, Arabs, Africans, or whatnot—surround a fort, prepare to make the final charge, and seem certain to send the "troopers" to their Maker. As the natives start to swamp the fort or overrun the wagon train or roast the settlers, we hear the blare of the trumpet and the roar of a herd of cavalry horses streaming across the plain to rescue the intended victims from the final onslaught.

Unfortunately, many procrastinators live with this wish. They hope for some salvation from doom to arrive as the eleventh-hour bell begins to toll. Sometimes it does. A boss may die of a heart attack the day a report falls due. A professor may take sick and cancel a final examination. A publisher may stop requesting the promised manuscript. Billing records at the phone company may get burned in a fire. Thus, sometimes long-overdue tasks never have to get done. But more often they hang like the sword of Damocles.

Overcoming-Self-Deception in Procrastination

Naturally you may not find it easy to overcome your self-deception and rationalization about procrastinating. The main reason for deceiving yourself relates to your shame about frankly admitting your procrastination; and unless you rid yourself of this kind of shame, your incentive to use *mañana* and other rationalizing excuses remains.

So start with this feeling of shame. At A, your Activating Experience, you procrastinate; and at C, your emotional Consequence, you feel ashamed of doing so; and, in addition, to hide this feeling of shame, even from yourself (or to avoid feeling it), you use various kinds of defensive maneuvers, such as those we have outlined in this chapter.

Okay—what do you tell yourself at B, your Belief System? You first tell yourself a sane set of philosophies, or rational Beliefs (rB's), such as: "I mainly defeat myself by procrastinating, and I don't like this kind of self-sabotaging behavior. I wish I didn't resort to it! How obnoxious! Why do I behave in this foolish manner?"

If you steadfastly stayed with these rational Beliefs (rB's), you would tend to feel disappointed with your behavior, sorry that you kept repeating it, and intent on trying to change it. And you would appropriately have these feelings—since you could give sensibly, empirically based reasons why you find it disappointing and disadvantageous to procrastinate and why you had better change that kind of behavior.

Foolishly, however, you tend to go on to, and to devoutly swear by, a set of highly irrational Beliefs (iB's): namely, "I *must* not procrastinate! I can't accept *myself* for giving in to this abominable behavior! No one can ever really like me and I'll never do anything well as long as I persist in it!" You *then* feel ashamed, depressed, panic-stricken, and completely slobbish.

Using RET procedures, and going on to D (Disputing), you can quickly and forcefully challenge your own nonsense: "Why *must* I not procrastinate?" Answer: "I can find no reason why I must not, even though many good reasons exist why I'd better not. If I live under conditions where I *do* procrastinate, including the conditions of my crooked thinking that lead me to do so, then under these poor conditions I almost certainly *must* procrastinate. So I'd better change the drafted conditions!"

Again: "Why can't I accept *myself* for giving in to this abominable behavior?" Answer: "No proof exists for the nutty proposition that I can't! If I choose to put myself down (as I clearly do) for procrastinating, then I obviously can choose *not* to put myself down for this behavior. My rating or not rating myself remains under *my* control; so I don't *have* to continue to deprecate myself, even if I keep procrastinating."

Again: "What evidence exists that no one ever will like me or that I'll never do anything well as long as I procrastinate?" Answer: "None whatever! I most probably will lose out by needlessly delaying important projects and will do some of them worse than I otherwise would. And some of my friends and associates probably will despise me if I don't get on the ball and stop this behavior. But I'll very likely do some things well and retain some friends even if I never stop it. So if I want better results, I know what to do. But even if I choose worse results for the rest of my days, I hardly turn into a slobbish, undeserving person. No, just a person who continues to act foolishly and self-damagingly!"

If you really discover and dispute your irrational beliefs about procrastinating in this manner, you almost certainly will lose your feelings of intense shame about it. You still will feel quite sorry about your inactivity. You still will feel motivated to try to change it. But you won't feel like a total worm who presumably *can't* change its ways.

The first step, then, in ridding yourself of defensiveness and self-deception about procrastination consists of acknowledging your feelings of shame about it, and of minimizing or eliminating these feelings with RET techniques. Second, you can take a look at the defensiveness itself and make yourself aware of it. When you have a *mañana* attitude for example, you can ask yourself: "Will I *really* start working on my assignment tomorrow? In what way will tomorrow prove better to work on it than today? By putting it off, won't I make it more difficult rather than less difficult? Wouldn't I find it much better if I did the assignment today and had a free day, to use whatever way I wanted, tomorrow? Won't doing it later give me too little time in which to get my materials together and then to write them up?"

Rationalizations, in other words, consist of reasons—albeit specious reasons—for doing or not doing something. And you always can analyze reasons, use the logico-empirical method to see whether they truly hold water. It seems amazing that humans resort to a rationalizing process, and that they do it almost automatically, with little or no purposeful learning involved. They do learn that a certain standard—such as doing things promptly—appears "right" or "correct." They conclude, with some learning involved here too, that they therefore *must* act correctly; and they feel ashamed or self-downing when they don't. So, recognizing that they would condemn themselves for their "incorrect" or "wrong" behavior, they frequently make up rationalizations, such as the *mañana* attitude in procrastination.

Fortunately, they have an additional amazing propensity—the ability to look at their rationalizations, to see them as just that, and to dispute and change them. So in case you use self-deceptive defenses to mask your procrastination, and thereby enable yourself to continue it, don't view everything as hopeless. You can undercut the core of your defensiveness by surrendering your feelings of shame, and you can see your self-deceptions and rationalizations and undo them.

Answering Some Common Rationalizations About Procrastinating

Because people make up so many different kinds of rationalizations to help themselves deny that they needlessly delay or to pretend that the needlessness of the delay really doesn't exist and that they have good reasons for postponing important things, we present here some of these rationalizations along with answers you can use to help yourself uproot and abandon them.

1. Rationalization: "I find it easier to do this task when I have to do it under pressure. So I will postpone it until the pressure builds up and then I can do it with ease."

Rebuttal: The task may *seem* easier when you have to do it under pressure, but usually you will find it harder under those conditions. For you then have to rush to complete it, cannot assemble all the relevant materials to help you do it well, have little time to look it over and review it, and often have to polish it off in a relatively unfinished, glossed-over manner. The "pressure," moreover, doesn't make you finish the task in the final analysis—*you* still do. You tell yourself, when you feel this pressure, "I really *have to* finish the task now." But you could tell yourself, long before such pressure mounts, "I'd really better finish the task now," and get just as good results. You *define* the conditions of doing the job as necessitating pressure. You really could do it under lots of other conditions—if you chose to do so.

2. Rationalization: "I don't know how to do the job properly. I'll wait until I know how before I do it."

Rebuttal: Hogwash! If you do know how to do the job—which you probably do—you have no legitimate reason for waiting. If you don't know how to do it properly, move your butt and find out how! Even if you don't know how to do it at all, you probably will learn much better by starting to do it than by sitting around and goofing.

3. Rationalization: "I hesitate to do this thing because I really don't want to do it."

Rebuttal: More hogwash! Your wanting to do the thing or not, once you have promised yourself and others to do it, has little relevancy. The less you want to do it, the quicker you'd better do it, as long as you have promised it. Then at least you'll have it out of the way! You probably mean by, "I really don't want to do it," "I shouldn't *have to* do it." Well, you don't really have to do it, in any absolute sense of that term. But since you contracted to do it, and presumably did so for your own good, you had better stop the nonsense and just do it. And it would seem nice if you really didn't have to do it at all and still could have the good results of doing it. But how likely does that seem? Highly unlikely! So you'd damned well better do it, whether or not you really "want" to.

4. Rationalization: "The world won't come to an end if I put this project off, so it really doesn't matter if I delay it."

Rebuttal: Quite right. The world probably won't come to an end if you put this project off, but that doesn't mean it doesn't matter if you do. Just because something doesn't rate as *all-important* doesn't mean that it has *no importance at all*. This project probably does have some real, though not sacred, importance to you and to others allied with you. Do it for its importance, its value, then, and not for its all-importance or holiness. Don't go from one foolish extreme to the other!

5. Rationalization: "I'll find this project easier to do when I feel in the mood. So I'll wait for that time, and do it then."

Rebuttal: It seems possible that a time will come when you'll feel in the mood to do this project, and that you'll then find it easier to do. Possible, but highly unlikely! The chances remain that (1) this time may never come; (2) it may come after the usefulness of doing the project has passed; (3) even if it comes in a reasonable period of time, the advantages accrued from waiting hardly will equal the advantages or ease you will get from doing it now; (4) if you work on the project now, when it doesn't seem so easy, you will overcome your inertia and it *then* will prove much easier than if you wait for ease to come naturally.

6. Rationalization: "I did it at the last minute once and it worked out well, so why not do it the same way again?"

Rebuttal: For several reasons: (1) Did it really work out well last time, or did you just get by without a disaster occurring? (2) Even if it did work out fairly well last time, wouldn't it have worked out better if you had not procrastinated? (3) Assuming that you got good results last time, even though you procrastinated, how about the extra pain, trouble, and tension you brought on yourself by delaying? Did your good result make *these* worthwhile?

7. Rationalization: "If I do this term paper at the last minute instead of right away, I won't have to spend too much time on it and will save myself a great deal of work and effort."

Rebuttal: Rot! The only time you probably will save by doing it at the last minute will get saved because you go at it in a rush and do it sloppily. If you did it well, or even adequately, it would take you no more time to do it at the beginning of the term than at the last minute. Even if you do save some time by doing it in a last-minute rush, you spend lots of time worrying, up to that point; you later tend to worry about how poorly you did because of rushing at the end; and you hardly enjoy any of the time you save before, during, or after doing the paper at the last moment.

8. Rationalization: "If I do this task right now, instead of putting it off till next week, I may never get the opportunity again to enjoy the encounter that I can enjoy tonight."

Rebuttal: False! You certainly *may* capitalize on a once-in-a-lifetime opportunity by doing something tonight and procrastinating on a task you have promised yourself to do. But you most likely will not. Many similar opportunities probably will present themselves after you have finished this task—and you will then have better conditions under which to take advantage of them. Quite likely, too, you will ruin many good opportunities for pleasure by procrastinating—for you will still have to work on your task long past the time when you otherwise would have completed it and will have to refuse opportunities that *then* come up. Moreover, as responsible people see you as an inveterate procrastinator they probably will reduce rather than augment the opportunities they throw your way.

9. Rationalization: "I would have gotten around to doing this sooner, but circumstances beyond my control prevented me from doing so."

Rebuttal: They did? More likely than not, *you* prevented yourself from doing so—perhaps even invented or exacerbated certain circumstances that you could then claim prevented you. Moreover, the more you procrastinate the more conditions likely will arise to interfere with your doing something. If you want to control or get around such interfering circumstances, do your tasks as quickly as possible.

10. Rationalization: "I've worked at this project for such a long time that I've lost all desire to do it."

Rebuttal: Quite right! Had you gotten to the project promptly and finished it, your desire to work at it probably would have persisted long enough. But because you kept putting it off and doing it in dribs and drabs, you have lost most of your interest in it. Besides, when you say you've lost your original desire to do it, you really may mean, "Because I view the project as so hard and keep delaying it—thus making it still *harder*—I *therefore* have lost most of my original desire to do it." If you stop the nonsense, get down to finishing the project quickly, and know that you will complete it in a reasonable period of time, your original zest may return!

11. Rationalization: "No one really cares whether I finish this task or not, so I may just as well keep putting it off."

Rebuttal: How do you *know* no one cares whether or not you complete it? Several people may care very much, but you may push their concern out of mind so that you more easily can continue your delaying tactics. And even if no one really does care whether or not you complete it—so what? You took on the project because you presumably wanted to do it or to get the results of having it done. If others don't care about your doing it, that remains their business. Why must anyone care, anyway? How does it help you to depend on other people's caring instead of on what you would like to do for yourself in life?

Summary

When you won't honestly face your procrastinating and try to erect defenses against it, you may resort to self-deceptions, such as the *mañana* and contingent *mañana* attitudes. These kinds of rationalizations work because of their assumed promissory nature. You decide to perform a task sometime in the future, so that you don't have to worry about it today. Actually, you decide only to put it off—not to fail to perform it at all.

By rationalizing and using other forms of escape from facing up to difficult problems, you usually add new difficulties. The incompleted tasks remain, and you waste energy inventing and maintaining your excuses for not doing them. Also, you often nag yourself for your delaying and your rationalizing.

Escapist "solutions"—including fantasy, media watching, overeating, listening to music, and reading at inopportune times—exacerbate the original problem and add further problems. Nothing seems to work but working! And, fortunately, just as you silently and unconsciously work first to procrastinate and then to deceive yourself about your delaying, you actively and consciously can work to undo both the procrastination and the defenses you erect to protect it. No matter how clever your rationalizations, your reasoning still can determine them!

11. Overcoming "Legitimate" Reasons for Procrastination

Although we may define virtually all delays in following through on an activity that you have decided on and plan to do as procrastination, this kind of definition has flaws. For the term *procrastinating* strongly implies that you have chosen to do a certain task and that you needlessly, foolishly, and consciously fail to carry it out in a reasonable period of time, or in accordance with the time schedule that you originally set.

We can think of at least seven mitigating factors that may contribute to your "normally" or realistically postponing certain projects that you have decided to complete. These include:

1. Naïveté or ignorance. Here you put off activities because you honestly think you cannot do them properly.

2. Fixed habits. You may tarry out of semi-automatic habits or patterns of delay that you follow because you feel comfortable giving in to such habits and do not realize that you could break them with some degree of effort, to establish new "easy" pathways.

3. Inertia. You have strong, and perhaps innate, tendencies to resist moving or acting when the time comes to shift from one endeavor to another.

4. Fallible memory. You may legitimately get distracted from your original goal or goals and forget to do what you have planned, or forget certain aspects of your plans whose oversight interferes with your completing a task on schedule.

5. Skill deficiencies. You may not have (or may have lost) the skill to carry out a plan promptly. Because of lack of ability or training, you may work more slowly, and require more breaks in your activity, than someone with more skill.

6. Physical interferences. You may have some unusual physical condition—such as illness or genuine fatigue—that impedes you.

7. Appropriate delays. You may wisely and appropriately

put off certain tasks—such as writing a paper—because more favorable conditions for doing them (e.g., the availability of a large block of time) may occur at some later period.

Although the foregoing reasons for procrastinating have some real legitimacy, the delay to which they often lead has distinct disadvantages. Let us see, therefore, whether you can devise and employ some methods of overcoming this "legitimate" kind of dallying.

Naïveté or Ignorance

You may procrastinate at beginning a task because you believe that you can't do it well, and that you'd better delay until you can do it better. Maybe you really *can* do it well enough right now. But you *think* you can't—so you "legitimately" put it off right now. Or you may think you can do a task well, but, because of your sex or position, you feel you "should" not try it; so you naïvely put off trying to do it.

Julie enjoyed mechanical objects and felt intrigued by how they worked. But her parents and friends saw her interest as most "unfeminine." Females, they said, "shouldn't" show interest in what makes a watch work, the electric lawn mower go or the car wheels move when its gears engage. Accepting these sexist views, Julie put off learning about mechanical things because the female role precluded her knowing about such matters. As a consequence, she felt guilty whenever she thought about reading books on mechanics. She also felt cheated when she watched her brothers work on the family automobile.

Not till years later did Julie realize that some women had mechanical interests similar to hers and that women might appropriately work with mechanical things. In a brief discussion with a female gasoline station attendant, she learned several women had enrolled in a course in mechanics at a local high school. Gleeful, she signed up and discovered that she could grasp the principles of mechanics even more rapidly than some of the more experienced males in the class.

Julie's procrastination clearly stemmed from ignorance. She bought what her parents and friends had told her without ever questioning their judgment. Accidentally, through new information and a new perspective, she initiated a career in auto mechanics which she previously thought didn't exist for women.

When your procrastination stems from naïveté or ignorance, you often can clear it up or ameliorate it by discovering what your lack of knowledge consists of and by remedying this deficiency. Suppose you want to take a certain course but hesitate to register for it because you think it has some prerequisites that you have not yet fulfilled and that the teacher of the course will not let you take it.

You obviously can check on these assumptions. Look in the school catalogue to see if it lists any prerequisite courses. Speak to your classmates, to see if they have taken this course and always have fulfilled these stated requirements. Talk to the teacher, even if you don't have the prerequisites, to see if he or she will make an exception in your case.

Whenever you assume that you have legitimate reasons for postponing an important project, check these reasons. Ask yourself: "Do I really have to put this project off? For what reasons? Why can I not get going on it now rather than later? Do specious elements exist in my 'legitimate' reasons for delaying? What could I do to make it possible for me to get to work promptly on the project, rather than assume that I have to postpone it?" When you ask, and honestly seek out the answers for, questions like these, many of your "good" reasons for delay will vanish!

Breaking Fixed Habits

If you keep procrastinating because you habitually act in slow-moving, now-you-do-it-and-now-you-don't ways, don't think you *have to* perpetuate such habits. Usually your breaking dysfunctional habits involves considerable difficulty, even if you feel highly motivated to do so. Breaking an excessive eating habit, for example, may prove exceptionally hard because you have established so many cues in your everyday life that you associate with eating, that you frequently stimulate yourself to overeat. These cues may include specific times of the day, the sight of the refrigerator, watching TV commercials that advertise food, or feelings of anxiety. Much compulsive eating also may occur so habitually that you may devour several pieces of chicken, a large bag of potato chips, a bar of candy, and several glasses of milk before you clearly recognize what you keep doing.

Developing desirable habit patterns, such as directly dealing with emotional troubles, or developing a program for increasing physical fitness, involves concerted effort and much practice. Developing an exercise habit means forcing yourself out of nonexercising patterns, perferably by practicing at specific times and places, so that the time and place serve as cues for beginning the activity. Overcoming overeating also requires much practice of new eating patterns to replace the old dysfunctional ones. This typically requires time and tolerance for backsliding, until your new patterns get stabilized.

A common belief exists that difficulties in breaking dysfunctional and establishing self-serving habits show you have weak character and "should" therefore psychologically trounce yourself. This idea can increase the probability of your procrastinating as you may bog down in self-castigation over setbacks rather than persist in doing your best to forge ahead.

Useful rules to follow in trying to break procrastination habit patterns include the following:

1. Assume that even if you have an innate tendency to act in an habitual manner, and even if you have practiced that habit for a good many years, you still *can* disrupt this pattern of behaving and substitute a less procrastinating pattern for it.

2. Don't put yourself down either for having the dysfunctional habit or for not working very hard against it. Your *behavior*, in this respect, may stink, but *you* don't rate as a stinker! Your habit patterns constitute only *parts* or *aspects* of you; they do not *equal* you!

3. Give yourself sufficient time to break a habit. Because you may have quite naturally created it and because you have practiced it for a fairly long period, you will find it almost impossible to give up quickly. Habits mean *accustomed* ways of behaving. And for quite a period ot time you probably will have to accustom yourself to different, newer habits before confirmed change takes place.

4. Allow for relapses! If you habitually dawdle today, but force yourself out of this pattern tomorrow, and even keep pushing yourself for a while, you still may fall back into dawdling later on. Don't feel surprised at this condition—it has a typically human quality! Accept your relapse with no self-condemnation, and get back to work at undoing the habit again . . . and again, and again!

Inertia

You won't always find it easy to switch from one activity to another. In writing this book, we often had trouble switching from one activity, such as listening to music, to another activity, such as working at the typewriter, and vice versa. Part of this inertia stems from personal absorption in the process of writing, and part of it from a natural tendency to resist changing actions.

The principle of inertia explains why, each time you work on a project, you may feel forced to exert yourself to re-initiate. For example, if you act shyly around strangers, and you consequently procrastinate about approaching them, you normally experience considerable inertia in pushing yourself to make approaches. You can keep forcing yourself to overcome this inertia by propelling yourself forward to socialize on many occasions. Doing so, you will usually feel increasingly comfortable and may even enjoy some of the self-propelling process. But you still will tend to fall back, at times, and experience some degree of inertia in meeting new acquaintances. If you ever rid yourself of all of it, that would practically amount to a miracle!

The general solution to the problem of procrastination caused or abetted by inertia therefore seems obvious. First, accept the fact that you naturally and easily hold back from many actions you would like to take. Second, refrain from downing yourself for having this "problem." Third, recognize that inertia constitutes a two-way, somewhat conflicting process: Once you have overcome it, it will tend to work *for* you and keep you engrossed longer than you may have expected in the project you resisted. So your initial inertia comprises a highly temporary, overcomable state. Fourth, if you throw yourself into new activities or changes without debate, and with an I-intend-to-get-going-come-what-may attitude, initial inertia tends to decrease and the discomfort of overcoming it seems minimal.

Dealing with the Frailty of Memory

You probably have a fallible memory, and can procrastinate because you genuinely forget things—rather than because you have sinister, hidden motives (such as psychoanalysts would hypothesize) and therefore deliberately *want* to forget. If you deem an activity (such as cashing a pay check before the weekend) highly important, you will tend to remember it better than a chore that you consider less important (such as writing a letter to a friend).

In the latter case, you easily could find yourself distracted by various everyday events. At the same time, if some unusually exciting opportunity transpires—such as having sex, conversing with a well-liked friend, or watching an enjoyable TV show—you can even distract yourself from check-cashing, and find yourself without money over the weekend.

If your memory tends to lapse seriously at times—and whose memory does not?—you can accept yourself with this kind of lapse and then make some suitable allowances for it. If you keep forgetting to study or to do your daily exercises, you can (1) set regular times for doing such tasks; (2) arrange for effective reminders like notes in the middle of your floor or on your bathroom mirror; (3) set alarm clocks or timers to let you know that the time has come to do the task; (4) keep check lists and review them periodically to see whether you have completed various things; (5) enlist friends or roommates to check with you at definite times to see whether you have done what you had promised yourself to do; (6) make some pleasurable things, such as eating, contingent upon completing some other things, such as doing your exercises. Don't make yourself ashamed to use all kinds of mnemonic devices to overcome some of the handicaps of a fallible memory.

Skill Deficiencies

You may find restarting a diet after several years of non-dieting difficult, as you may have to relearn previously learned dietary techniques. If you want to make a comeback as an athlete, you may require considerable practice to bring yourself to your former skill level. If you take an advanced mathematics course years after the basic courses, you may expend considerable effort in relearning old material before you safely can go on to newer material. If you start up a new business, you may discover that it takes more time than you first imagined to achieve competence at it. In all the above examples, your skill deficiencies rather than procrastination would primarily delay your accomplishing your objectives.

Arthur discovered that his part-time business entailed far more time and work than he originally had estimated. Thus, he fell behind not only in developing it, but in other areas of his life. He decided, however, to accept this situation, anticipating that he probably would manage his affairs better once he gained more business experience. Meanwhile he did his best and saw his temporary inefficiency as the price he had to pay to gain the skill he desired.

Sometimes you hardly can avoid wrong estimates about how long it will take to complete a job. If so, your falling behind in your work or recreational activities may not represent procrastination, but merely fallible prediction.

You can usually overcome skill deficiencies with additional training. If you procrastinate about studying because you lack study skills, you can take a course or read books on the subject, ask your friends how they manage to study better, talk with your teachers about increasing your skills, or use other means. By applying yourself, you can augment your skill considerably and remove much of your motive for procrastinating about studying, learning to drive, and engaging in other skilled pursuits.

Physical Factors

We all have frailties of the body. Illness, infirmity, chronic disorders (such as muscular dystrophy, headaches, simple fatigue, or variations in hormonal or blood-sugar levels) can delay performance. A week of illness can set back your carefully planned schedule—even force you prematurely to terminate some projects. You would best uncomplainingly live with debilitating physical factors—better not expect to give a super-performance when feeling ill, fatigued, or physically agitated.

General physical conditions may influence perceptions. Thus, when physiologically upset, you may tend to perceive the world more negatively than after a good night's sleep or a hearty meal. When you have low stress tolerance, you may more easily overreact. But your bodily states mainly set the stage for your psychological reaction; they rarely *cause* it. The *meaning* you ascribe to such states largely determines how you will behave.

If you wake up with a headache, you may not appreciate new budding flowers popping out of the ground on a spring morning, because you focus upon how dreadful it feels to have the headache. Indeed, you may aggravate the headache by focusing upon it. If you then receive an important call, after ten minutes of intensive discussion on the phone, you may practically forget about the headache!

When lying in bed after you have had a tooth pulled, you may concentrate more on your pain than on trying to fall asleep. You *could* focus on more pleasant thoughts. The focus of your thoughts and perceptions can promote considerable pain or relief, depending upon how you *view* your situation.

At times in the menstrual cycle, some women experience a sense of depression and inertia which they would prefer to attribute to external happenings in their lives, feeling all the more irritated when they can't come up with an environmental explanation for their low level of functioning. One woman came to her therapy session depressed about once every four sessions. Her depression coincided nearly 100% with the onset of her period and, once she recognized this, she still felt slightly down, but much relieved compared to the times when she had no explanation for her depression. Rather than preoccupying herself trying to discover external explanations, she forced herself to continue at lowered efficiency with her projects, ceased to ask herself, "Oh, why do I feel so depressed," thereby avoided procrastinating and did pretty well.

I (W.K.) feel agitated and quite irritable about two days prior to getting secondary symptoms from a virus, or after going nearly a day without eating. I (A.E.) have diabetes and act drunkenly and bizarrely when I fail to balance my daily shot of insulin with sufficient food. When either of us observes agitation or irritability, we realize that something has gone physically wrong and we take action to overcome the effects of the virus or to correct our eating patterns. Otherwise, we tend to avoid important issues and to procrastinate.

You need not always know the cause of every affective experience; indeed, you may have some feelings whose origins you never learn. Too bad! Worrying about unknown causes can lead to procrastinating, as you then lose time ruminating rather than acting. And you'd better make realistic allowances for agitating physical states. You won't act as a super-performer under all conditions. After all, you have human, not godlike attributes. You therefore have natural physical limitations which serve as barriers to perfect efficiency.

You frequently can eliminate or compensate for physical factors that lead to legitimate procrastination. If you take good care of your health and use whatever means you have to improve it, you will tend to suffer less from morning inertia, diabetes, menstrual difficulties, or other physical impediments to work. If you obtain regular medical checkups, you will make yourself more aware of your physical disabilities and increase your ability to eliminate or deal with them. Knowledge increases your power in this respect; and the determination to use your knowledge to deal with your physical handicaps gives you even more power over your body and its impediments to promptly and efficiently carry out projects.

Accepting Appropriate Delays

You can learn to distinguish between appropriate and inappropriate procrastination. As a student, you may tend to worry about putting off studying for tests but you may also find times when you do rather well with last-minute cramming. If you can do so without bringing about appreciably lower grades or needless anxiety, you need not view your procrastination as wrong or self-defeating.

When can you logically and appropriately put off important projects? That depends on several factors. If you forget things quickly, last-minute cramming rather than studying for days or weeks in advance of an exam may save you some time and trouble. If you truly work better in spurts of massed time, holding off doing a term paper for the last week of the semester may work fine.

But specious rationalizations hardly equal valid reasons. Don't try to fool yourself into believing that you logically can put things off when you really can't. And look for alternative, nonprocrastinating solutions before you cavalierly give in to postponements. If you'd better mass your efforts at assigned papers, how about trying some *advanced* massing? You then stand much less of a chance that illness, unavailability of reference materials, or other factors beyond your control will sabotage your last-minute endeavors.

Consider each case of "legitimately" putting things off on its own merits and firmly ask yourself, "Do I really have a good reason for this particular procrastination—or does my reason serve as a clever rationalization? What makes the present postponement truly appropriate and logical? Maybe

I'd better discuss it with a more objective friend, to see whether I deceive myself."

Summary

Technically, procrastination simply means putting off something until a future time, postponing or delaying action. As such, it sometimes appears quite legitimate. You may, out of ignorance or naïveté, needlessly delay when you think that action remains impossible or impractical. You may tarry because of semi-automatic habits that you cannot immediately control or block. You suffer from real inertia, which prevents you from doing things as quickly as you would like to do them. You may also procrastinate because of your fallible memory, as a result of skill deficiencies, or because of physical interferences.

Although you cannot completely surmount these "legitimate" forms of procrastination, generally you can ameliorate them. First, you can recognize them and the reasons for their occurrence. Second, you can stop downing yourself for giving in to them and stop ranting against the world for inflicting you with them. Third, you can persist at modifying or removing them. Fourth, you can expect setbacks from time to time and not let yourself get thrown by them. Fifth, you can work at increasing your frustration tolerance and accepting the elements of procrastination that remain after you have coped with the removable ones.

Watch your tendency to rationalize and to confuse legitimate with illegitimate reasons for delay. You may not always distinguish precisely between the two. But if you keep trying, you mostly will!

12. Verbatim Psychotherapy Session with a Procrastinator

I (A.E.) took the following verbatim transcript from a first and only therapy session with a client who came with the problem of procrastinating on her doctoral thesis in the field of sociology. At age thirty-five she felt she had various emotional difficulties, but only one motivated her to seek therapy—the problem of her not finishing her dissertation. Since neither she nor the therapist speak in E-prime (although the therapist uses it in his writing, as in the present book), the dialogue consists of regular English. This client had read *A New Guide to Rational Living* and had familiarized herself with the concepts of RET.

THERAPIST: What problem would you like to talk with me about?

CLIENT: I, uh—I have been, for the past two years, writing my doctoral dissertation. And procrastinating all over the place.

THERAPIST: Yes?

CLIENT: I find more reasons for not finishing that paper—uh, valid reasons to me. But I'm just not finishing it, and I probably would do much better if I finished it.

THERAPIST: All right. So at C, a Consequence, we start with procrastination. After, at A, you have, we'll call this Activating Experience, an assignment to do your doctoral thesis, in order to get the degree—which we assume you want. Right? Okay, so according to my theories, it's B which is the issue. About the assignment, A, you have a perfectly sane, though negative, Belief—B. A rational Belief about that assignment. Now, what do you think that Belief is?

152

CLIENT: Well, that it is work. It will—

THERAPIST: Right.

CLIENT: It will require that I put effort into it. And it is an assignment the I don't exactly relish.

THERAPIST: Right. You have the obser—

CLIENT: I'd rather not do it.

THERAPIST: Right. You have the observation, "It is work. It is effort." And then the evaluation, "I don't like that. I'd rather not do that work. What a pain in the ass!" Now, suppose you *only* stayed with that rational Belief about the work. "I'd rather not do it. What a pain in the ass! I wish I didn't have to do it. But that's the way it is—a pain in the ass." How do you think you'd feel and how would you behave, at C, if you *only* stuck to that rational Belief?

CLIENT: Fine. I'd probably do it. Because it, it just would be perhaps uncomfortable and something I don't want to do. But, uh—

THERAPIST: Right.

CLIENT: —it would be no more than that. Apparently, it's become more than that.

THERAPIST: Right. In other words, you'd probably feel sorry and disappointed. But you'd also feel sorri*er* and disappointed*er* about *not* doing it. You'd do a hedonic calculus there. And therefore you'd probably do it. Is that right?

CLIENT: (Nods head in affirmation.)

THERAPIST: But we know that you're procrastinating, you're goofing, you're inert. Right? Now, what nutty, irrational Belief do you seem to have in addition to "What a pain in the ass! I don't like it. I wish I didn't have to do it."? There's a nutty Belief there, in all probability. Now, what do you think that is.

CLIENT: It's, it's a firm belief that I shouldn't have to do it.

THERAPIST: Right. Cherchez le *should*—and you can almost always get one immediately. And yours is probably, "I *shouldn't* have to do this obnoxious thing." Or, "Because it's a pain in the ass, they shouldn't require it of me." Right?

CLIENT: (Nods affirmatively.)

THERAPIST: And you could say, by extension, "And it's awful that they do! And I'll be goddamned if I'm going to do it—when I shouldn't have to!" Something like that. All right. Now we go to D, Disputing: "*Why* shouldn't they? What is the reason that they shouldn't require this obnoxious thing of me—writing a thesis to get my union card?"

CLIENT: There really isn't any. Uh—

THERAPIST: But? Yes, "there isn't any reason why they should. *But*—"

CLIENT: —they shouldn't!

THERAPIST: "But they shouldn't!" Right. All right, now why *shouldn't* they? Let's go back to the question.

CLIENT: Oh, it's unanswerable. Because, of course, they *can* require it.

THERAPIST: They can—and they *should*. Because anything that exists, in that sense, *should* exist. Let's assume it's a hundred percent unfair. They stupidly, unfairly require it, this thesis. If that's what they're doing, they *should* do it. Is that correct?

CLIENT: Well, in the terms of, uh, your philosophic stand, they should. But I have the belief that they shouldn't. This is what I keep telling myself.

THERAPIST: And where would your belief lead you?

CLIENT: To procrastinate right out of it.

THERAPIST: That's right! To procrastinate, or do it in 1997, or something like that. You see, as long as you're saying, one, "It's unpleasant, and I don't want to, but I'd *better*," and then, two, "But I won't. They *shouldn't* do it to me," you'll get more procrastination. So your activity, or inactivity, is *consonant* with your belief. Is it going to be very possible for you to stop procrastinating while you believe, "They *shouldn't* do this to me"?

CLIENT: No, I'd have to stop believing that.

THERAPIST: In all probability. You could force yourself to do it *in spite of the belief*, but that would be very hard. And so far you haven't done that. So it's possible. But it's unlikely you will. Or it's unlikely you'll do it in any reasonable length of time. And the time might pass, they might throw you out of the program. How long do you get to complete it?

CLIENT: Oh, five years. But three of them have passed.

THERAPIST: Right. So in another two years, if you keep up that, "They *shouldn't* do this to me!" and they think, "We damned well *should*!" you may get thrown out of the program. So that belief causes your rebelliousness, your inertia, your procrastination—*and* leads you to results you don't want. Therefore, you'd better—you don't *have* to—but you'd better do what?

CLIENT: Change the belief about what's going on.

THERAPIST: That's right! Give up that *Belief*. Now one way, we're already saying, you really ask yourself, very *vigorously*, "Why the hell *should* they?" And you said before, "There's *no* reason." But I heard you say that in a very namby-pamby manner.

CLIENT: That is, *cognitively* I realize that there is no reason why they souldn't ask me to do it. But there's a disagreement between what I *understand* and my *feelings*.

THERAPIST: Well, that's one way of putting it. But I'd rather put it more precisely: "*Cognitively*, once in a while, *lightly*, I realize that they should. But cognitively, most of the time, *strongly*, I realize that they *shouldn't*." You've got two conflicting cognitive beliefs. And one is *weaker* than the other, and you're *acting* on the stronger one.

CLIENT: Which is the belief, "They shouldn't!"

THERAPIST: Yes, "They shouldn't do this to me! *Because* it's so unpleasant and *because* it's such a nutty system, etc.—they shouldn't!" So when you say, "I *understand,* cognitively, that I, that they *should,*" you really mean, *"Once in a while, lightly,* I understand that." You see, and that can be proven very simply. Suppose we have the simple model which I often give, of the black cat; and you come to me and you say, "Well, black cats are unlucky." And I say to you, "Well, that's a nutty, magical belief. Prove that they're unlucky." And you think about it and you say, "Well, hell, I guess they aren't unlucky. No, come to think of it, they're damned well not unlucky—black cats. They won't cause me any unusual harm. They won't scratch me more than a white cat or blue cat." And then a black cat approaches and you run like hell, and your hair bristles. Now, what's your *real* belief?

CLIENT: Black cats are unlucky.

THERAPIST: Right! Now, you still have—at times—a focus on, "Oh, no, they're really not." But most of the time you believe *much more strongly,* "But they *are!*"

CLIENT: Until it comes time to sit down and write the paper, I'm saying, "I believe they *should.*"

THERAPIST: That's a good point! Right now you're saying to *me,* "Well, you know, I guess they should require the thesis." But when it's unpleasant, when you're sitting down to write the paper, when that onerousness is there, you're saying, "But those bastards *shouldn't!*"

CLIENT: Right! (laughs)

THERAPIST: Right. "They *shouldn't!*" Now, they're both cognitive beliefs. And when you say, "I have *emotional* insight or feeling, which says "They shouldn't" and cognitive or intellectual insight, "They should," you're part lying to yourself. Because the so-called "emotional" insight or feeling is the result of a strong cognition. That's why I use the black cat illustration. Because you can think *two* things about the black cat. Now your problem is to *admit* your real, majority, stronger belief is, "They shouldn't!" And your mild, occasional belief, especially when you're not doing the thesis, is, "They should. It's too damned bad, but they *should* demand it. I'll do it." Now your problem is to *increase*, to put more steam behind, the weaker belief and to *decrease* the stronger one.

CLIENT: In what way do—in what way would you advise that I do when it comes time to leave here, I go home, and I do have a couple of hours which I could use to sit down and do it? And then I start believing, "But they shouldn't be requiring it"?

THERAPIST: Well, I'd advise two or three things. But the first thing I'd advise is to *act* against the procrastination-creating belief. People don't realize that when they act *by inertia* in favor of a belief how much they really are strongly *favoring* it. The black cat again, just as an illustration. If you say to yourself, "Well, I guess black cats aren't unlucky," but, everytime you're about to go to a neighborhood of black cats, you refuse to go, or you think of visiting a friend with a black cat and you refuse to visit, what propaganda are you feeding yourself by the refusal?

CLIENT: That you had better stay away! That—

THERAPIST: Yes, "Because they *really are* unlucky!" You see, every time you *don't* approach the black cat, you very strongly confirm your superstitious belief. And people don't realize that just because they're *not* doing something, they don't see that that's a *confirmation* of a magical belief. You see. So what I would do, *one* thing I would do, is every single time, practically, when you really have an hour or two—let us suppose you could work on the thesis. No horseshit! No matter how unpleasant it feels, force yourself to do it. *Partially* in order to give up the belief—not just to finish the thesis. That would be one good reason. But *to give up the belief.* And you could use, for this forcing, incidentally, operant conditioning. You know what operant conditioning is? The principles of self-management?

CLIENT: Reinforcement.

THERAPIST: Yes, reinforcement. Let me—It merely means you take the behavior, now—we'll get back to the cognition in a minute—just the behavior of doing the thesis, which you're now avoiding, and you reinforce it when you do it, you reward yourself. And you penalize yourself—not *damn* or *punish* yourself—just penalize yourself immediately and quickly, when you don't avoid. For example, what do you *like* to do in life, that you do practically every day?

CLIENT: I have a hobby that involves cats. I raise cats—different breeds.

THERAPIST: And practically every day you have something to do with the cats? And you enjoy that? You do that spontaneously and enjoy it? Okay. Let's keep that in mind. And what do you hate to do that you avoid doing?

CLIENT: The thesis!

THERAPIST (laughs): Aside from the thesis. There are other things—and we can't too well use the thesis to penalize your not doing the thesis. But what else do you hate to do—some activity that you tend to avoid because you find it obnoxious?

CLIENT (pause): Well-I have a professional responsibility to, uh, evaluate my sociology students in the one class I now teach. And I avoid this, I find it obnoxious.

THERAPIST: I see. You avoid speaking to them and giving out an evaluation?

CLIENT: Writing out a formal evaluation.

THERAPIST: Okay—writing out one. All right. So you could set yourself a schedule. What would be a fair schedule of the hours per day or week you could work on the thesis?

CLIENT: I probably—if I worked at it—I could probably find at least an hour and a half a day.

THERAPIST: Okay. So let's just say an hour and a half. Now if tomorrow you do the hour and a half a day, by twelve midnight or whatever it is, the next day you allow yourself to be with the cats. If you don't do it, no cat companionship! See—no contact with the cats. And if you *don't* do it, then you sit down and write, whatever you choose as a penalty—one, two, or three evaluations. Immediately! And you thereby immediately reinforce yourself and penalize yourself for the writing and the nonwriting behavior. In regard to the thesis. Which will just *help* you do it. And the more you do it, the more you'll tend to contradict the procrastination-causing idea. Because, you see, once you procrastinate, which in RET we call C or Consequence, you tend to get *another* C about that. You tend, like most people do, to turn that first C, procrastination, into an A or Activating Experience. You say to yourself, "Now, at A, I'm procrastinating." Now how do you feel *about* your procrastination?

CLIENT: Guilty.

THERAPIST: Right. Guilty, downing—

CLIENT: Ashamed.

THERAPIST: Because, at B, what are you saying to create the guilt or shame?

CLIENT: "Well, I shouldn't—I shouldn't procrastinate, and I am—"

THERAPIST: Right. And therefore that *makes* me—

CLIENT: A rotter or a turd!

THERAPIST: Right. So you're using your symptom, procrastination, to down yourself about. And you waste time and energy in this kind of self-downing. So you could also say, at D, "Even if I keep procrastinating, what makes me a worm? And what would the answer be?

CLIENT: "Nothing—except my *belief* that I am."

THERAPIST: That's right! And you could give that up—which would help you. But every time you work against it—And you also, incidentally, conclude. "A rotter like me *can't* stop herself from procrastinating!" You get that nutty idea, too. So every time you *force* yourself to work against it, you'll sabotage that nutty idea. You won't easily give up the whole idea, "I'm a worm if I do procrastinate," for that idea you partly maintain whenever you go back to the procrastination and think you mustn't. But at least the idea, "I can't do it. I can't stop myself from procrastinating"' That idea gets knocked in the teeth if you force yourself, even at times, to do the thesis.

CLIENT: Suppose I set up a reinforcement schedule, as you suggested, and then I begin to procrastinate about the reinforcement. I keep taking care of my cats every day, even though I *don't* work on my thesis.

THERAPIST: Right. Then that brings us to a related belief, which we've not emphasized so far and which would be a good thing to consider. Because then you would probably be convincing yourself, "*If* I do the hard work of only reinforcing myself when I do the thesis, then I'll probably change my ideas and change my behavior—about the procrastination. But, rationally, I don't like that. I find that obnoxious— to penalize myself or fail to reinforce myself in order to bring about change."

CLIENT: Yes, I don't want to get change that hard way.

THERAPIST: But what are you saying to yourself, *irrationally,* about the penalties and the rewards you can use to help yourself change? Not only, "I don't like them," but what else are you saying?

CLIENT: "I *should* have my rewards and I *shouldn't* have penalties."

THERAPIST: Yes. And, "I *can't stand* penalizing myself or failing to reinforce myself! It's *too* hard! The system would work, reinforcement, operant conditioning; but it's too hard—and it *shouldn't be* that hard!" But why the hell *shouldn't* it be that hard?

CLIENT: Because I don't *want* it to be!

THERAPIST: Right! And *you* run the universe! Right?

CLIENT: I'd like to think it! (laughs)

THERAPIST: Well, where's the evidence that you do? I'm a scientist. I haven't noticed you running the universe! If you did, that thesis would *do* itself!

CLIENT (Laughs): Touché!

THERAPIST: Yes, and it isn't doing itself. *You're* doing yourself! See? So you have another nutty idea—about the thesis—low frustration tolerance, "It's *too* hard! It shouldn't *be* that hard!" And about the reinforcement—or the changing, we can call it. "Yes, I know I could change and stop procrastinating. But it's too hard to use the reinforcements and penalties. It's easier to procrastinate." Is it—really?

CLIENT: No, because you go around with this, uh, guilt or whatever?

THERAPIST: But even without the guilt. Let's suppose you just had a feeling of irresponsibility, not guilt—you merely told yourself, "I act wrongly by procrastinating," instead of "Because I wrongly procrastinate, I am no damn good as a total person," would it be easier to procrastinate than not?

CLIENT: Well, historically, I felt it is easier. Because I've been doing it.

THERAPIST: At any given moment, you find it easier. As you're about to do the work—the hour and a half of it—you see that it's easier *not* to. But then it still is there. You have it hanging over your head. You won't get the degree. You may *never* get the degree. Now in terms of any *real*, or total, pleasure-pain calculus, *is* it easier?

CLIENT: No.

THERAPIST: It's easier in the *short run*. But harder in the long run! Now, if you would keep showing yourself, "Yes, it is easier *right now*,"—what practically every alcoholic says, or drug addict—"It's easier *right now* to cop out. But in the *long run* it's harder." Which is what these addicts *don't* say, but what you can show yourself. And then you won't find it that "easy." It's easier for me, as a diabetic, to eat sugar than not eat it. Because it tastes good. But I make myself acknowledge that in the long run it's going to do me in. So I don't eat it. See? So one thing you can do—just to get back to it—is the operant conditioning on the behavior, which will help you change your thinking. Now, the second thing you could do is rational-emotive imagery, which I'm going to give you right now. Because you could change your thinking about the procrastinating (1) while you're procrastinating, really work it through: "Why is it *too* hard, the thesis? Why *shouldn't* I have to do it?" and change it—force yourself. (2) After you've procrastinated, the next day, the next hour, you could say, "Well, I did badly. But why do I have to keep doing so? I can force myself to unprocrastinate, and change my philosophy next time, tonight or tomorrow." So you can do it then. Or (3) beforehand—you can actually tackle it before the procrastination comes up. So let's try No. 3, beforehand. Close your eyes and imagine, right now, that you really have the hour and a half to do your thesis in. It's tomorrow, and you have the hour and a half and you could do it. You have two or three hours and you have an hour and a half in which to do the thesis; and it would be better if you did it. You know that, in the long run. *But* it *is* a pain in the ass! And there *are* more enjoyable things you could do right then—either eat, go to the movies, play with your cats, etc. Now you're picturing that: You could do the thesis, but it's a royal pain in the ass to do it. Right? And how do you feel, honestly, about doing it, under those conditions?

CLIENT: It's almost like a kind of disgust.

THERAPIST: Right. You feel disgusted about doing it. Okay. Now, keep that same picture, get with the feeling of disgust, and then change your feeling right now to disappointment, instead of disgust. Just disappointment—frustration. No disgust. Now, can you do that?

CLIENT: Yes, momentarily.

THERAPIST: All right. Now *how* did you do that?

CLIENT: Well I just, I just said, "It isn't disgusting. It's just a pain. I can do it, though it's a pain."

THERAPIST: "It's only a pain in the ass. I don't like to do it. But I *can*. And I'll probably get rewards for doing it."

CLIENT: But the feeling went away, right away—right back to disgust.

THERAPIST: Right. Because? That's what you practice—disgust. Now, your rational-emotive imagery homework assignment is: Every day for at least ten minutes, in the morning or afternoon, when driving your car, or doing something that you can do and still think about other things, you *practice* (1) that picture—that you really would better do the activity, the working on the thesis for an hour and a half, and (2) let yourself feel disgusted at this image, because you do find it unpleasant. And then *change the feeling,* for a few seconds, a few minutes, to *only* disappointment, only frustration. And really *work* at changing it—the same way you just temporarily did it: by saying sort-of, "Well, it isn't the end of the world. And it won't kill me. And it's a pain in the ass. But that's *all* it is, a pain in the ass." The same way you just did. *Practice* that for at least ten minutes every day. And if you don't practice it, incidentally, you can use the operant conditioning or self-management technique to get yourself to do the practice. You only allow yourself to play with your cats *after* you do the ten minutes of practice; and penalize yourself, writing a couple of evaluations out if you don't do the practice. You see? But you're *practicing* now, every day practicing, feeling disgusted!

CLIENT: Yes, I see.

THERAPIST: Great practice! You see, you just *make yourself* feel more and more disgusted. Just like *practicing* playing the piano wrongly. Well, if you do, you'll get very adept at playing it wrongly! And you're very adept at making yourself feel disgust—in addition to displeasure. Now, we're trying to get you to feel only the disappointment, the sorrow, the regret, the displeasure, the frustration *without* the disgust—so you can then feel the frustration and displeasure of *not* doing the thesis. For that's going out of your mind. The disgust you feel about doing the thesis is outweighing the disappointment and displeasure of *not* doing it. It's a powerful feeling, the disgust, which you're practicing.

CLIENT: So this session has been a reinforcing one. So let's say that for the next week I have, I work at it.

THERAPIST: Right.

CLIENT: And then I find I'm trailing off.

THERAPIST: Right.

CLIENT: Because I don't have any reinforcement like you.

THERAPIST: All right. But what would you be telling your-self, to trail off? Let's suppose, for example, that for a week you do it, and you really get an hour and a half of work on the thesis done a day. How much closer to finishing your thesis would you be? How many hours would it take to do it altogether, by the way?

CLIENT: Finish it?

THERAPIST: Yes.

CLIENT: Not much. It's almost—Maybe about a hundred hours.

THERAPIST: Right. So you see it would only take about eighty days or perhaps seventy-five days to finish. But let's suppose in a week you fall back. Now what would you be telling yourself to make yourself fall back?

CLIENT: I'm back to, "I shouldn't have to!"

THERAPIST: Yes, "It's too hard! I shouldn't have to!" So you could go right back to contradicting, to disputing that. You're saying, "I don't have to do the work on the thesis." And you *don't* have to. But then you're going to get the results, the bad results of not doing it. And you'd better ac-knowledge (1) these bad results of not doing the thesis and (2) the fact that you really *do* have to—or at least, would damned well better—do it if you want the good results of getting your Ph.D. degree.

CLIENT: I see.

THERAPIST: Or you could use a stiffer penalty for not working on the thesis. I have a stiffer penalty I've just invent-ed for people to use to help themselves do difficult tasks, which practically always works. Unfortunately, most people won't adopt it. But when they accept and enforce this penalty, they almost always lose weight, or do thesis, or whatever they find very difficult to do. I read about it in one of the behavior therapy journals. You go to the drug store and you buy some asafetida, or other vile-smelling substance, and you make yourself smell it every time you don't work on your thesis. Or, another variation on this, is to get some ipecac, which is an emetic, and will make you vomit every time you take it; and you force yourself to take a dose, every time, again, you fail to do an hour and a half's work on the thesis. But I have recently used, with several clients, a better one than that, or one that works better for many people. Every day that you don't do an hour and a half of work on the thesis, you take a hundred-dollar bill and you burn it—yes, burn it. You'd be surprised, if you really use this and enforce it, how many hour and a halfs you do!

CLIENT: What's the name of that stuff you get in drug stores?

THERAPIST: You see! You can practically always arrange something obnoxious that you make yourself do if you don't work on the thesis; and if it is unpleasant enough, and you really do it immediately after you fail at your contract with yourself to do the work, you'll soon start doing it!

CLIENT: I can well believe it!

THERAPIST: I originally got ideas like this not only from the behavior therapy literature but also from a movie I once saw while flying on a plane to the West Coast. This fellow in the movie gets captured by the Rebels during the Civil War. He's not a soldier but he supplies the Union Army with food and other produce. So he gets caught by the Rebels, and they say, "Oh, now that we've caught you, you'll supply us." "Oh, no," he replies, "I'm loyal to the Union. I'm not going to do that." So the Rebel chief shoots off one of his fingers. And he says, "I'm going back to see you every day for the next nine days, and you'll have another finger missing each day if you don't decide to supply us." Now how long do you think it took this fellow to start supplying the Rebel army?

CLIENT: One day, I hope!

THERAPIST: That's right! He quickly decided to live with nine fingers, instead of with eight, and then with seven, and then with six, and finally with none. So, actually, you can always set up stiff penalties. And if you fall back, after first working on your thesis for some days, you would be refusing to enact such stiff penalties. *But*—you'd then be bringing on yourself a worse penalty. See, it really would be better for you to burn a hundred-dollar bill for a few days—for that would be really obnoxious, in all probability; but you'd get your thesis done pretty quickly to avoid further penalties like this.

CLIENT: Very quickly!

THERAPIST: That's right! You see. And, incidentally, you never have to burn any money. That's the beauty of it. People say, "Oh, I couldn't do that—burn a hundred-dollar bill." But I say, "But you don't *have to*. You merely do the thesis instead."

CLIENT: That might work. I'll consider trying that.

THERAPIST: I highly recommend it!

CLIENT: Will you help me with another belief I have about my thesis?

THERAPIST: Sure.

CLIENT: I don't know whether it's true or not. But I believe it. I happen to believe that the advisor I have is extremely tough. The belief I've carried around for about two years is that he is worse than almost any advisor I have ever had contact with or any of my colleagues have had.

THERAPIST: Let's suppose that's true. Let's suppose he is. That's all the more reason for getting your thesis done quickly!

CLIENT (laughs).

THERAPIST: You see, I'm assuming that you can't get rid of him.

CLIENT: No.

THERAPIST: No. So he's rigorous and you can't get rid of him. So you'd better quickly get from out his rigor—out from under his rigor—by finishing it. So your belief about his being this way may be correct. Are you thinking that it is an incorrect belief?

CLIENT: No. I believe it is correct. But I can see someone else saying, "Oh, you're just saying that because he's rigorous to *you*."

THERAPIST: Oh. No. I think you have two beliefs: One is, "He's more rigorous than any professor I've ever known." And two, "He *shouldn't* be!"

CLIENT: Yes. That I definitely have!

THERAPIST: All right. Now, why shouldn't he be *more* rigorous than any professor you're ever likely to encounter?

CLIENT: No, I now see he should. But what I have been saying to myself is, "Because he is blocking me from getting something I want."

THERAPIST: No. He is blocking you from having a ball while you write the thesis and talk it over with him. If he's that rigorous, he'll give you a painful time. But he's not blocking you from writing the thesis. And actually, as I've said, it's the same principle—you're stuck again on your silly *shoulds*. Suppose you have to eat a certain meal and it has seven courses; and you just have to eat it all—some experiment or something like that is taking place. And one of the courses is obnoxious. Now, what would be a wise thing to do?

CLIENT: Eat the obnoxious course first.

THERAPIST: That's right. Get it over with. And then leisurely eat the rest of the meal. So if he really is this obnoxious, if he acts obnoxiously, get to him as often and as quickly as possible—and then you won't have to have him much longer as an advisor. This way, you've had him for three years. Well, if you do the thesis, you'll have him for five years—and then out! Now you can get rid of him, according to you, in about seventy-five days or so. Why not fix it only at seventy-five days, if he acts that obnoxiously? See, so it's the second belief—"He *shouldn't be* that way!" Hogwash!

CLIENT: I see.

THERAPIST: Do you really see? Why does your belief, "He shouldn't be that way!" amount to hogwash?

CLIENT: Because he has every right to be the way he is, even though I don't want him to be that way. I can't tell him how to be.

THERAPIST: And no matter how unfair his rigorousness is, and how much you dislike it, and how much it impedes your progress on your thesis?

CLIENT: He still has that right. I can't *make him* fair. Unfairness *does* exist in the universe. I'd better put up with it.

THERAPIST: And thereby be fairer to yourself than you now are! For no matter how unfair he is, you are still more unfair. For he thinks that he is being a fine—in fact, probably a great advisor—by sticking to his rigorousness.

CLIENT: Oh, he really thinks he's helpful.

THERAPIST: I'm sure he does. Anyway, he doesn't recognize his presumed unfairness to you. But you do see how unfair it is for you to keep yourself from finishing your thesis. And you still stick to that form of gross unfairness! How about that?

CLIENT: Oh, I see now. I'm *really* unfair to me. Much more than he is. I see what you mean.

THERAPIST: Good. Now if you'll only give up that goddamned "He shouldn't be that way!" you'll immediately start treating yourself much more fairly.

CLIENT: You know, you're right. Treat *myself* much more

fairly—and in that way at least try to make up for some of his unfairness. A much better plan!

THERAPIST: Exactly. Why don't you try *that* plan?

CLIENT: Yes.

THERAPIST: Anything else you want to ask me about this problem?

CLIENT: No, that about covers it.

THERAPIST: Okay. You see if you can think it over and do some work along the lines we've discussed today. Try it and see!

Although my vigorously disputing, even actively arguing with, the client's basic irrational beliefs occurred in a direct, no-nonsense manner, and constituted the kind of approach that most psychoanalytic, client-centered, relationship-oriented, and other therapists would probably view with horror, it worked beautifully in this case. I saw this client six months later at one of the regular Friday night workshops which I give at the Institute for Rational Living in New York City (and where I interview people in public and try to get some resolution of their emotional problems in a single session with me and some of the members of the audience) and she reported complete success with her procrastination on her thesis.

The day after she spoke with me, she instituted the program I suggested of reinforcing herself for doing and penalizing herself for not doing an hour and a half's work per day on her dissertation. She also began to work vigorously against her *shoulds* and *musts* about doing it and about the rigorousness of her professor. She finished the entire thesis in about seven weeks, obtained her degree, and felt very good about her accomplishmnt. She has used RET on herself with some of her other problems since that time and teaches some elements of it to all her sociology classes.

A single session, plus reading of *A New Guide to Rational Living* and some of my other books, plus some very hard work on her part, and she stopped procrastinating. She also, though she did not specifically focus on this problem, stopped her procrastinating about giving evaluations to her students and began to work more promptly at several other things in her life that she had previously self-defeatingly kept putting off. But best of all, as she reported to the Friday workshop group, "I have reduced my *shoulds* and *musts* to a degree that I can hardly believe. I try more than ever to change the unpleasant events of my life and to make them better. But if I can't, I can't. Tough—but hardly awful!"

References

We have included in the following list of references the main books and articles we consulted in writing this volume, as well as useful materials in the general field of self-help. We have placed a check mark (√) in front of items that readers may wish to delve into further in their search for some of the elements of rational living. We have placed an asterisk (*) before items that readers may order from the Institute for Rational Living, Inc., 45 East 65th Street, New York, New York 10021. The Institute will continue to make available these and other materials, as well as to sponsor talks, seminars, workshops, and other presentations in the area of human growth and rational living. Those interested can send for its current list of publications and events.

√ Adler, A. *Understanding Human Nature.* New York: Fawcett World, 1974.

√ Adler, A. *What Life Should Mean to You.* New York: Putnam, 1974.

Ainslie, G. Specious reward: a behaviorial theory of impulsiveness and impulse control. *Psychological Bulletin,* 1975, 82, 463–96.

*√Alberti, R. E., and Emmons, M. L. *Your Perfect Right.* San Luis Obispo, Calif.: Impact, 1973.

√Ard, B. N., Jr. *Counseling and Psychotherapy.* Palo Alto, Calif.: Science and Behavior Books, 1976.

Arnold, M. *Emotion and Personality.* New York: Columbia University Press, 1960.

Bandura, A. *Principles of Behavior Modification.* New York: Holt, Rinehart and Winston, 1969.

Baudhuin, E. S. Rational Emotive Therapy and general semantitherapy: a review and comparison. *ETC.,* 1975, 32, 195-202.

Beck, A. T. *Depression.* New York: Hoeber-Harper, 1967.

Beck, A. T. Cognitive therapy. *Behavior Therapy*, 1970, 1, 184-200.

*√Beck, A. T. *Cognitive Therapy and the Emotional Disorders*. New York: International Universities Press, 1976.

*√Bedford, S. *Instant Replay*. New York: Institute for Rational Living, 1974.

*√Berger, T. *I Have Feelings*. New York: Behavioral Publications, 1970

*√Blazier, D. *Poor Me, Poor Marriage*. New York: Vantage, 1975.

Bourland, D. D., Jr. A linguistic note: writing in E-prime. *General Semantics Bulletin*, 1965-1966, 32-33, 111–14.

Bourland, D. D., Jr. The semantics of a non-Aristotelian language. *General Semantics Bulletin*, 1968, 35, 60-63.

Corsini, R. J., and Cordono, S. *Role Playing in Psychotherapy: a Manual*. Chicago: Aldine, 1966.

DiLoreto, A. *Comparative Psychotherapy*. Chicago: Aldine, 1971.

Dollard, J., and others. *Frustration and Aggression*. New Haven: Yale University Press, 1939.

Dubois, P. *The Psychic Treatment of Nervous Disorders*. New York: Funk and Wagnalls, 1907.

Ellis, A. Outcome of employing three techniques of psychotherapy. *Journal of Clinical Psychology*, 1957, 13, 334–50.

Ellis, A. Rational psychotherapy. *Journal of General Psychology*, 1958, 50, 35-49.

*√Ellis, A. *Reason and Emotion in Psychotherapy*. New York: Lyle Stuart, 1962.

Ellis, A. *Homosexuality*. New York: Lyle Stuart, 1965.

*√Ellis, A. *The Art and Science of Love*. New York: Lyle Stuart, and New York: Bantam Books, 1969.

*√Ellis, A. *How to Master Your Fear of Flying*. New York: Institute for Rational Living, 1977.

*√Ellis, A. *Sex Without Guilt*. Rev. ed. New York: Lyle Stuart, and Hollywood: Wilshire Books, 1972.

*√Ellis, A. *Executive Leadership: A Rational Approach*. New York: Citadel, 1972.

*√Ellis, A. *Growth Through Reason*. Palo Alto, Calif.: Science and Behavior Books, and Hollywood: Wilshire Books, 1973.

*√Ellis, A. *Humanistic Psychotherapy: The Rational-Emotive Approach*. New York: Julian Press, and New York: McGraw Hill Paperbacks, 1974a.

*√Ellis, A. *The Sensuous Person*. New York: Lyle Stuart, and New York: New American Library, 1974b.

*√Ellis, A. *How to Live with a "Neurotic."* Rev. ed. New York: Crown, 1975a.

*√Ellis, A. *Disputing Irrational Beliefs*. Leaflet. New York: Institute for Rational Living, 1975b.

Ellis, A. On the disvalue of "mature" anger. *Rational Living*, 1975c, 10(1), 24-27.

*√Ellis, A. *Sex and the Liberated Man*. New York: Lyle Stuart, 1976.

*√Ellis, A. *The Intelligent Woman's Guide to Mate-Hunting*. Rev. ed. New York: Lyle Stuart, 1978.

Ellis, A. *How to Live With—and Without—Anger*. New York: Readers Digest Press, 1977.

Ellis, A., and Grieger, R. *A Sourcebook of Rational-Emotive Therapy*. New York: Springer, 1977.

Ellis, A., and Gullo, J. M. *Murder and Assassination*. New York: Lyle Stuart, 1972.

*√Ellis, A., and Harper, R. A. *A Guide to Successful Marriage*. Hollywood: Wilshire Books, 1971.

*√Ellis, A., and Harper, R. A. *A New Guide to Rational Living*. Englewood Cliffs, N. J.: Prentice-Hall, and Hollywood: Wilshire Books, 1975.

Ellis, A., and Sagarin, E. *Nymphomania: A study of the Oversexed Woman*. New York: Manor Books, 1974.

*√Ellis, A. Wolfe, J. L., and Moseley, S. *How to Raise an Emotionally Healthy, Happy Child*. Hollywood: Wilshire Books, 1972.

√ Epictetus. *Enchiridion*. Indianapolis: Bobbs-Merrill, 1970.

Eysenck, H. J. *Experiments in Behavior Therapy*. New York: Macmillan, 1964.

Ferster, C. B. Nurnberger, J. I., and Levitt, E. E. The control of eating. *Journal of Mathematics*, 1962 1, 87-109

Franks, C. M. (Ed.). *Behavior Therapy: Appraisal and Status*. New York: McGraw-Hill, 1969.

Friedman, M. *Rational Behavior*. Columbia: University of South Carolina Press, 1975.

*√Garcia, E., and Pellegrini, N. *Homer the Homely Hound Dog*. New York: Institute for Rational Living, 1974.

Goldfried, M. R., Decenteco, E. T., and Weinberg, L. Systematic rational restructuring as a self-control technique. *Behavior Therapy*, 1974, 5, 247-54.

√ Goldfried, M. R., and Davison, G. *Clinical Behavior Therapy.* New York: Holt, Rinehart and Winston, 1976.

√ Goldfried, M. R., and Merbaum, M. (Eds). *Behavior Change Through Self-Control.* New York: Holt, Rinehart and Winston, 1973.

*√Goodman, D., and Maultsby, M. C., Jr. *Emotional Well-Being Through Rational Behavior Training.* Springfield, Ill.: Thomas, 1974.

√ Greenwald, H. *Direct Decision Therapy.* New York: Aronson, 1975.

*√Grossack, M. *You Are Not Alone.* Boston: Marlborough, 1974.

Harper, R. A. *The New Psychotherapies.* Englewood Cliffs, N.J.: Prentice-Hall, 1975.

*√Hauck, P. A. *Overcoming Depression.* Philadelphia: Westminster Press, 1973.

*√Hauck, P. A. *Overcoming Frustration and Anger.* Philadelphia: Westminster Press, 1974.

*√Hauck, P. A. *Overcoming Worry and Anxiety.* Philadelphia: Westminster Press, 1975.

*√Hauck, P. A. *The Rational Management of Children.* New York: Libra, 1967, 1974.

Hauck, P. A. *Reason in Pastoral Counseling.* Philadelphia: Westminster Press, 1972.

Homme, L. *How to Use Contingency Contracting in the Classroom.* Champaign, Illinois: Research Press, 1969.

Horney, K. *Collected Writings.* New York: Norton, 1972.

Jakubowski-Spector, P. Facilitating the growth of women through assertive training. *Counseling Psychologist,* 1973, 4, 75-86.

Jourard, S. *The Transparent Self.* Princeton, N.J.: Van Nostrand, 1964.

√ Kanfer, F. H., and Goldstein, A. P. *Helping People Change.* New York: Pergamon, 1975.

√ Kelly, G. *The Psychology of Personal Constructs.* New York: Norton, 1955.

*√Knaus, W. J. Overcoming procrastination. *Rational Living* 1973(2), 2-7.

*√Knaus, W. J. *Rational Emotive Education.* New York: Institute for Rational Living, 1974.

√ Korzybski, A. *Science and Sanity.* Lancaster, Pa.: Lancaster Press, 1933.

*√Kranzler, G. *You Can Change How You Feel.* Eugene, Ore.: Author, 1974.

*√Lange, A. and Jakubowski, P. *Responsible Assertive Behavior*. Champaign, Illinois: Research Press, 1976.

√ Lazarus, A. A. *Behavior Therapy and Beyond*. New York: McGraw-Hill, 1971.

√ Lazarus, A. A. *Multimodal Therapy*. New York: Springer, 1976.

√ Lazarus, A. A. and Fay, A. *I Can If I Want To*. New York: Morrow, 1975.

Lazarus, R. S. *Psychological Stress and the Coping Process*. New York: McGraw-Hill, 1966.

*√Lembo, J. *Help Yourself*. Niles, Ill.: Argus, 1974.

√ Lembo, J. *The Counseling Process*. New York: Libra, 1976.

Lindsley, J. R. On the value of mature anger. *Rational Living*. 1975, 10(1), 24-27.

√ Mahoney, M. *Cognition and Behavior Modification*. Cambridge: Ballinger, 1974.

√ Mahoney, M. J. and Thoresen, C. E. *Self-Control: Power to the Person*. Monterey, Calif.: Brooks/Cole, 1974.

√ Marcus Aurelius. *Meditations*. Baltimore: Penguin, 1971.

*√Maultsby, M. C., Jr. *More Personal Happiness Through Rational Self-Counseling*. Lexington: University of Kentucky Medical School, 1974.

*√Maultsby, M. C., Jr. *Help Yourself to Happiness*. New York: Institute for Rational Living, 1976.

*√Maultsby, M. C., Jr. and Ellis A. *Rational Emotive Imagery*. New York: Institute for Rational Living, 1975.

*√McMullin, Rian, and Casey, Bill *Talk Sense to Yourself*. Lakewood, Colo.: Jefferson County.

√ Meichenbaum, D. *Cognitive Behavior Modification*. Morristown, N.J.: General Learning Press, 1974.

Meichenbaum, D. Self-instructional methods. In Kanfer, F., and Goldstein, A. (Eds.). *Helping People Change*. New York: Pergamon, 1975.

Meichenbaum, D. A self-instructional approach to stress management. In Spielberger, C., and Sarason, I. (Eds.), *Stress and Anxiety in Modern Life*. New York: Wiley, 1975.

*√Moore, R. H. *The Rational Living Vignette Series: Subscriber Handbook*. Clearwater: Florida Branch of the Institute for Rational Living, Inc., 1975.

Moreno, J. L. *Psychodrama*. Beacon, N.Y.: Beacon House, 1970.

*√Morris, K. T., and Kanitz, H. M. *Rational-Emotive Therapy*. Boston: Houghton Mifflin, 1975.

Mosher, D. Are neurotics victims of their emotions? *Etc.*, 1966, 23, 225–34.

Perls, F. C. *Gestalt Therapy Verbatim*. Lafayette, Calif.: Real People Press, 1969.

Piaget, J. *Judgement and Reasoning in the Child*. Totowa, N.J.: Littlefield, Adams, 1970.

Premack, D. Reinforcement theory. In Levine, D. (Ed.), *Nebraska Symposium on Motivation*. Lincoln: University of Nebraska Press, 1965.

√ Raimy, V. *Misunderstandings of Self*. San Francisco: Jossey-Bass, 1975.

√ Rimm, D. C., and Masters, J. C. *Behavior Therapy*. New York: Academic Press, 1974.

Ringenbach, P. T. *Procrastination Through the Ages, a Definitive History*. Palmer Lake, Colo.: Filter Press, 1971.

√ Russell, B. *Conquest of Happiness*. New York: Bantam, 1969.

Schacter, S. *Emotion, Obesity and Crime*. New York: Academic Press, 1971.

Skinner, B. F. *Beyond Freedom and Dignity*. New York: Knopf, 1971.

√ Stuart, R. B., and Davis, B. *Slim Chance in a Fat World: Behavioral Control of Obesity*. Champaign, Ill.: Research Press, 1972.

*√Tosi, D. J. *Toward Personal Growth. a Rational-Emotive Approach*. Columbus, Ohio: Merrill Publishing Company, 1974.

Trexler, L. D. A review of rational-emotive psychotherapy outcome studies. Paper presented at the First National Convention on Rational Psychotherapy, Glen Ellyn, Illinois, June 6, 1975.

Velten, E. A laboratory task for induction of mood states. *Behaviour Research and Therapy*, 1968, 6, 473–82.

√ Watson, D. L., and Tharp, R. G. *Self-Directed Behavior*. Monterey, Calif.: Brooks/Cole, 1972.

√ Wolpe, J. *Psychotherapy by Reciprocal Inhibition*. Stanford, Calif.: Stanford University Press, 1958.

*√Young, H. S. *A Rational Counseling Primer*. New York: Institute for Rational Living, 1974.

Index

ABOUT THE AUTHORS

Dr. Albert Ellis, born in Pittsburgh and reared in New York City, holds a bachelor's degree from the City College of New York and an M.A. and Ph.D. degrees in clinical psychology from Columbia University. He has practiced psychotherapy, marriage and family counseling, and sex therapy for over thirty years and continues this practice at the Institute for Advanced Study in Rational Psychotherapy in New York City, where he also serves as Executive Director.

Dr. Ellis is the author of *Sex Without Guilt, How to Live With A Neurotic, Executive Leadership: A Rational Approach, A New Guide to Rational Living,* and *The Sensuous Person* (Signet), among many other books.

Dr. William Knaus is in the private practice of psychotherapy in New York City and Springfield, Massachusetts. He is the executive director of the Fort Lee, New Jersey Consultation Center, and teaches in the graduate division of American International College. Dr. Knaus has published numerous articles for professional journals on positive preventative mental health programs for children, on procrastination, and on therapeutic strategies for practicing clinicians. Since 1965, Dr. Knaus has actively served as the supervisor of hundreds of psychotherapists and counselors. He is an industrial and clinical consultant and the author of *Rational Emotive Education* and *Do It Now.*

More Reading from SIGNET and MENTOR

SIGNET Books of Special Interest

Buy them at your local

bookstore or use coupon

on next page for ordering.

SIGNET and MENTOR Books of Interest